HOW TO PROFIT

FROM...

Car Boot Sales

M+S

MeS

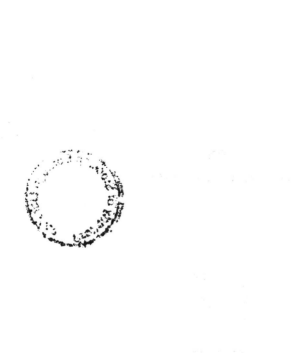

HOW TO PROFIT FROM...
Car Boot Sales

BY
FIONA SHOOP

REMEMBER WHEN

First published in Great Britain in 2009 by

REMEMBER WHEN PUBLICATIONS
An imprint of
Pen & Sword Books Ltd
47 Church Street
Barnsley
South Yorkshire
S70 2AS

ISBN 978 1 84468 048 1

A CIP catalogue record for this book is
available from the British Library

Printed and bound in Thailand
By Kyodo Nation Printing Service, Thailand

Pen & Sword Books Ltd incorporates the Imprints of Pen & Sword Aviation,
Pen & Sword Family History, Pen & Sword Maritime, Pen & Sword Military,
Wharncliffe Local History, Pen & Sword Select, Pen & Sword Military
Classics, Leo Cooper, Remember When, Seaforth Publishing and
Frontline Publishing

For a complete list of Pen & Sword titles please contact
PEN & SWORD BOOKS LIMITED
47 Church Street, Barnsley, South Yorkshire, S70 2AS, England
E-mail: enquiries@pen-and-sword.co.uk
Website: www.pen-and-sword.co.uk

CONTENTS

INTRODUCTION

I WROTE my first ever article on car boot sales over 20 years ago, at
a time when no one really approved of them or thought they would
last. It was like airing your laundry in public, instead of giving it to
charity or throwing it away, as was the norm back then. How times
have changed. Since 2003, I have been a regular columnist for *Car Boot
and Fairs Calendar* – a must-buy publication for anyone interested in
car boots, not for my column, but for the directory at the back of the
magazine, showing what's on, where and when. I was also an antiques

Fiona Shoop filming Boot Sale Challenge *in Dorchester.*

expert on *Boot Sale Challenge* but was too successful and had to be asked to lose. I refused because it wasn't about winning, it's about knowing how to make a profit and what's worth buying. I've been an antique dealer since 1982, have written well over 4,000 articles on antiques and collectables, as well as several books. I've given lectures, worked as a consultant and been on several other TV shows, always saying the same thing – you can make money from other people's junk. All you have to do is know what to spot and how much to pay – then where to sell it. It's easy. In theory!

What I loved about *Boot Sale Challenge* was being paid to do what I really enjoy: rummaging through other people's belongings and finding what other people have missed. I also love buying for myself and was constantly having to be hauled back to film whilst nosing through boxes of treasures, often buying toy cars for my lovely nephew, Zed. Admittedly, he didn't actually get to play with all of them, as there are some fantastic finds amongst old toys. I also got to buy retro furniture and accessories for my house and a whole host of other goods for far less than I'd expect to pay at antiques fairs, shops and auctions. Then there were the curtains and sheets which I used for styling in magazines – a prop shop would have charged me £5-20 each just to borrow them and I'd have to pay fines for any stains. The front cover and dozens of pages of several food magazines were filled with my bargains, not just material but all those props – stylish antique porcelain, crystal goblets and bowls, even cutlery, all for virtually nothing. You can make a living that way. Some antique dealers don't even do fairs anymore, they make their money at car boots – for a fraction of the stall rent and only working half-days. It's the perfect way to earn a living or just extra income for a holiday, home improvements – or whatever you want. It's all there.

There's the jewellery, the furniture, the computer games – everything you could ever need or want, all for less than you'd have to pay in shops, even charity shops nowadays. And car boots are fun. They're fantastic places to while away a weekend whilst making money. Oh, there are some things which aren't great about them but that's why I'm here. I've been going to car boots and writing about them for over 20 years. I've discussed them on TV and radio, in newspapers, magazines and in chapters of books. But now, for the first time, I'm sharing everything you need to know about car boots in one handy book. There's even a directory at the back so you can keep it in your car and make extra money, not just at weekends but all through the week. And it's easy money – all you have to do is read on....

Fiona Shoop
Car boot expert and antique dealer

CAR BOOT BASICS

CHAPTER 1

WHAT EXACTLY IS A CAR BOOT SALE?

C AR BOOT sales are not all the same. It's been years since I went to one which was just that – places, generally fields, where people sold off their unwanted household goods. They're more businesslike now, with market traders (fruit and veg, electronic accessories, stationery etc.) and antique dealers, new furniture sellers, even the RAC have been known to stall at car boots. And you don't need a car. Look around and there are people who've been dropped off earlier and are just stalling with a table and chair. There are vans galore, even motorbikes. Oh, and few people actually sell directly out of their car boots anymore; most of us just lean against them or hang clothes over them.

All types of people stall out – dealers, market traders, people wanting to make a bit of extra money at weekends, others who want to clear excess belongings. House clearance firms sell a lot of the low-end goods at the sales and use it for networking, to get more business. People clear unwanted goods after family members die. There are lots of different sellers with different reasons for being there.

Times have changed. We no longer give everything to charity or the dump. We're more aware, thanks to programmes like *Life Laundry*, *Cash in the Attic* and *Everything Must Go* (I

Earn enough money to be in the pub in time for a Sunday roast. This 1950s bar at Denham car boot was a fraction of the price you'd expect to pay at an antiques fair.

You can earn a living by selling at car boots, as this professional dealer does. The jewellery cabinet, as well as the quality of her goods, set her apart from the other pitches at this Thursday car boot in Sussex.

worked on all of them) that there's money in lots of old tat. Charity begins at home, now more than ever. Charity shops, in my opinion, are not what they were. I find them expensive and I've been deterred from giving goods to charity by the behaviour of some of the people who work there, especially those who refused goods after dad died and behaved appallingly. Charity shops cannot afford to be snobs in the current climate, not with car boots and eBay, but they need to learn that. I give to charity but I now do it direct, with money. Why give hundreds of pounds worth of goods to one shop in one go when they complain that I've given them too much stuff or have signs in the windows ignorantly announcing, 'No car boot goods'? Enough of a moan, but it's one of the reasons car boots do so well.

And it's instant money; eBay is great but you have to wait a few days for the auction to finish before you get your money, pack the goods, go to the Post Office and all the rest. Car boots are cash in hand – although the tax man is aware of them. Indeed, in some places (such as Scotland, Newcastle and Kent, see p113) you need to register if selling at car boots like a business and not just occasionally to clear excess goods. But, if you're lucky, you stall out in the morning and spend your earnings on a lovely roast lunch at the pub by 1pm. Again, that might just be me but that's what I love about them – half days for good money.

A car boot is a way to sell goods and get money for them. They take place in fields, hard-standings, airfields and the fields of stately homes. There are even indoor car boots, which seems a bit wrong but at least they don't rely on the weather. Above all, car boots are a great, fun way to make a profit.

Discover a bargain or earn an extra income in your spare time – whatever your needs, you'll find the answer at car boot sales.

CHAPTER 2

WHAT ARE THE PROS AND CONS OF CAR BOOTS?

A S WITH all things, there are positives and negatives of buying and selling at car boots. Many of these points are general and there are exceptions to every rule. Some dealers are there every week, some can offer guarantees which are genuine and not all car boots happen at weekends. If in doubt, ask before buying.

Car boots are an easy way to earn extra money or even start a new business – if you know how.

When buying

There are pros and cons when buying at car boots, depending on what you're buying:

Pros

- Items are generally far cheaper than other sources, e.g. retail shops, second-hand shops, antiques fairs and centres, auctions and even many charity shops. This applies not just to collectables but clothes, books, CDs, electrical goods, furniture, pet accessories and books.

- The potential profit can be huge if buying from non-experts, e.g. people clearing out their own homes, some house clearance businesses or general dealers – and you could make tens of thousands or more from a bargain buy.

- Car boot sales are great for buying children's clothes and toys, which are generally expensive to buy new and rarely last for long – especially baby clothes as babies grow so quickly.

- Some sellers are there every week and will help to source exactly

Enjoy a day out with the family and discover some great bargains along the way. And to think some people thought car boots were a storm in a teacup!

what you're after, whether it's a quality rose bush which they guarantee will grow (or your money back) or an electrical item. For professional car booters, loyalty and reputation is as important as it is for retail shops. Just ask for their phone number when buying or thinking about buying.

- It's a fun event and a great way to spend a weekend morning. Entrance is either free or cheap – expect to pay from nothing to £1. Compare that to most antiques fairs, where entry fees run from around 50p-£20 (the latter being exceptional).

Cons

- There are generally no guarantees. If the goods are broken, you have no recall. (There are exceptions to this rule amongst the market-trader elements.)

- Apart from some regulars, you don't know if you'll see the seller again, so if you want to change an item or it goes wrong, you have no redress. Something which doesn't actually work isn't the bargain it appeared to be and you've lost your money.

- If buying clothes, you generally can't try them on first to see if they fit.

- Electrical goods, in particular, can be dangerous. Professional car booters often demonstrate that they work before selling them.

- Things have got much better since regular raids on car booters by Trading Standards but pirated goods are still available at many events, especially DVDs (see p36 and 74).

Poynton car boot in Sussex when the rain started. Don't forget to pack your patience when leaving car boots, you'll need it.

- You might end up parking quite a distance from the event at larger car boots, which can be difficult when carrying heavy or awkward pieces, and it can be difficult to move closer to collect goods.

- You can get stuck in traffic jams entering or leaving the venue. With experience, this is easily overcome, as you learn the best time to arrive and leave to avoid time-consuming, frustrating jams.

Pitch rent is much cheaper than the stall rent at antiques fairs. This dealer paid around £10 for a double-sized pitch. Expect to pay at least five times as much at an antiques fair and that really cuts into your profit margins.

WHEN SELLING

There are pros and cons when selling at car boots, depending on your needs, e.g. as a business or just clearing unwanted belongings for space or to raise money:

PROS

- Space is cheap – much cheaper than antiques fairs or markets (e.g. £6-8 versus £20-30+).

- They finish early so you can be home for lunch, instead of at antiques fairs or markets where you're expected to stay all day.

- You can clear unwanted belongings and get paid for them instead of giving them away for free or paying someone to take them away. A lot of house clearance firms now expect to be paid for clearing goods, even ones worth money. Ten years ago, they'd always pay you for the job but now they can charge. It's not cheap – up to £500, depending on what you need clearing – and then they sell your goods and make even more money.

- If you do house clearance yourself, car boots are a great way to offload items which aren't good enough for antiques fairs or auctions but too good for the dump.

- People will buy virtually anything, so turn your junk into money.

- Antique dealers find car boots more profitable than summer antiques fairs, where trade slows down as buyers – especially the public, as opposed to fellow dealers – don't want to be inside when the sun is shining.

- Antique dealers can often clear lower-end stock for more money at car boots than they could at fairs and also pay less rent for only half a day's work.

- When you're used to it, it's a fun and sociable way to make money and clear goods.

- It can offer extra, regular income – useful when paying for summer holidays or unexpected bills.

Cons

- Buyers can be rude if you're new to car booting or that particular car boot.

- Haggling can be aggressive and might not be to everyone's taste.

- Novice car booters can find it overwhelming – for example, when buyers try to 'unload' your car for you.

- You are expected to pay tax on your car boot income, even if you only stall out a couple of times (or once, as the tax man would say).

- If you stall more than a couple of times in some counties (e.g. Lancashire, see p113), you can be fined if you're not registered as a dealer, even if you're just clearing your house and it's taking longer than expected.

- Car insurance companies have been known to check car boots to look for regular dealers and see if they and their vehicles are listed along with their employment. If not and you have an accident, they could refuse to pay out, as it's seen as fraud not to declare another form of employment (e.g. market trader or antique dealer), even if it's only part-time but regular.

- It can be difficult to leave early if the car in front or behind is too close. Again, with experience, there are ways to prevent this from happening.

- At larger venues, you can get caught up in traffic jams at the end of the event if you haven't snuck out early. Check first, as not all car boots allow sellers to leave before a certain time.

You could waste a day and your pitch rent if it rains. This field at Sayers Common in Sussex was already waterlogged when I arrived, promising that some cars would need towing out before the end of the event. Check before travelling during bad weather to see if a car boot is still on.

CHAPTER 3

WEATHER REPORTS

T HE WEATHER is one of the main problems with car boots. You do need to check the forecast before stalling out or travelling far for buying. Some car boots will get cancelled if it's too wet, not just because there won't be many buyers but because cars can get bogged down in the fields.

Organisers will leave an answerphone message saying if events have been cancelled. This does happen on a regular basis. Apart from anything else, the people who own the fields don't want them churned up so they won't be useable for weeks. A bit of rain is fine, a deluge is bad for business.

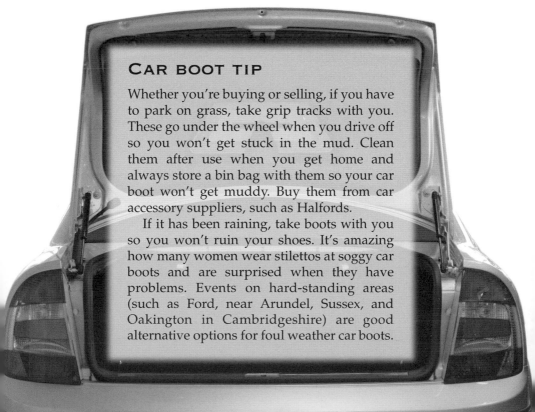

CAR BOOT TIP

Whether you're buying or selling, if you have to park on grass, take grip tracks with you. These go under the wheel when you drive off so you won't get stuck in the mud. Clean them after use when you get home and always store a bin bag with them so your car boot won't get muddy. Buy them from car accessory suppliers, such as Halfords.

If it has been raining, take boots with you so you won't ruin your shoes. It's amazing how many women wear stilettos at soggy car boots and are surprised when they have problems. Events on hard-standing areas (such as Ford, near Arundel, Sussex, and Oakington in Cambridgeshire) are good alternative options for foul weather car boots.

If you're going to be a regular car booter, invest in some gripper tracks from car accessory shops so you don't get stuck in the mud. This waterlogged scene was from the car boot car park at the start of a rainy day. Some organisers will cancel events to prevent problems with cars getting stuck and the fields getting torn up by tyres.

If you're expecting showers, think ahead. If stalling, don't leave out anything which would be ruined, e.g. paper goods including pictures, record covers and ephemera such as posters and magazines. Keep them in the car boot where they can be seen by buyers. Put tarpaulin, bin bags or a cloth over the stall when the rain starts and remove it carefully afterwards, so you don't end up wearing the water. We've all done it! Don't forget the ink will have run on any paper labels, so you'll need to change them when it's dry. And if the rain won't let up, pack up and go home. Your buyers will have done so.

I wrote an article for *Car Boot and Fairs Calendar* about the weather because we are at the mercy of it when it comes to car boots and even antiques fairs. But a little bit of rain is a good thing when you're a buyer as the sellers – especially those selling unwanted goods – just need to get rid of their belongings and will drop their prices. That's where you profit.

Snow is also an issue. In theory, most car boots won't be affected by this because they generally don't start until the spring (although there are exceptions to the rule and there are year-round car boots). But, with the weather more unreliable than ever, just check before travelling.

SUN STROKE

And then there's the sun, which you wouldn't think would be a problem, but it's all down to being sensible. On sunny days, wear sun protection cream, a hat and, if you need them, sunglasses. Drink plenty of water. This does clash with my advice on p145 but it's

Hot days are perfect for car boots but don't forget the sun cream and treat yourself to an ice cream. Most of the mid-range and large car boots have them on sale.

sensible as you don't want to get dehydrated. I've had sunburn and sunstroke on what I thought were fairly mild early summer days. Just be prepared and if you are liable to get sunstroke (fair complexion or red hair and freckles), take a hat. If you have a dog with you, be aware that it might not drink water which has been kept in the car on too hot a day as I discovered – and then had to buy bottled water for the thirsty dogs. Just take the water container out when you arrive and keep it in the shade. For hot summer days, I always keep my own bottled water in the freezer the night before a fair (removing a bit to allow for expansion). I take it out first thing, so by the time I come to drink it, I have chilled water. It does make a difference when you're working in the sun and probably talking more than normal as you sell goods.

CHAPTER 4

GENERAL ADVICE AND WARNINGS

THESE are general points for both buyers and sellers. There are chapters with advice targeted at buyers on p85 and for sellers on p155. For now, these are issues which everyone should know about before going to a car boot.

ARRIVING

If you can, always arrive early so you have a good position, whether you're buying and don't want to have to carry goods far and can leave easily, or selling and need a good selling spot with plenty of room. Late arrivals get crammed in, so get there early. Never trust the advertised start time. One car boot used to open at 6.30am and not the 9am advertised, so bargains and good parking spots had disappeared by the time some buyers arrived. This meant 'late' sellers had smaller spaces than the early ones, with many buyers already gone by the time they got there around the official start time. Ask the sellers in the front positions what time it really opens. You could ask the organisers as well but in this case, they told me 8am as they didn't want everyone getting there early. For this reason, always try to visit a car boot before selling there for the first time. If you arrive slightly after the real start time, whether buying or selling, expect to queue.

Always have your pitch rent or entry money ready – exact change only – to avoid wasting time when there is a busy queue. The boards outside the venue often state pitch and entrance fees. Larger venues expect both buyers and sellers to pay as they drive in; smaller ones charge the buyers as they go through the gates on foot. Some are free. So whether you're selling or you're a buyer, have a handful of money ready on arrival. I have a small pile of change ready in my car just in case it's pay on driving and not on walking into the venue.

In the car

Some of these points are geared more to buyers but there are certain items all car booters need to have in their car:

- Strong carrier bags for collecting your buys. Not all sellers have enough or any at all, so be prepared. Sellers should keep their plastic supermarket bags (if there are still any in future) and use them to give the goods to buyers.
- Wrapping, keep newspaper handy for ensuring goods are wrapped when sold or get home safely when bought. If buying china, also keep bubble wrap in the car. However, I'd advise that you don't take it with you when walking around as the seller might think you've spotted something of exceptional value and up the price!
- Take a box or two in the car so goods don't slide around on the way home. If a seller, boxes make loading easier.
- Take cloths to cover your buys in the car if they don't all fit in your boot or if you need to take the seats down to make extra space. This way, thieves won't be tempted.
- Water, carry it around with you as a buyer to avoid overpriced drinks at the venue. Plus you don't have to waste time queuing. If a seller, especially in hot weather, don't get dehydrated (but see 'toilets' p31).
- Food, again, avoid queues, especially if you're selling and shouldn't be away from your stall or don't want to miss out on those must-buy bargains.

Food and drink

The last thing you want is to waste your change on unnecessary costs or cram your body with salty goods such as the ubiquitous bacon butties. They only mean you'll get dehydrated quicker, which in turn means you'll need to waste timing queuing again for drinks and then – the very worst point about car boots – for the toilet. Food and drink at car boots is of differing quality but mostly fried and, in my opinion, over-priced. Take sandwiches with you or a snack and then treat yourself to a decent lunch afterwards. Take your own water as well and save time and money. I always make an exception for the ice cream van, especially on hot summer days, even though prices and quality are no more than you'd expect. But who can resist an ice cream or ice lolly if they're allowed them? Just watch your timing, though, as queues can get long. Wait until it's quiet, so you don't queue when you could be buying bargains.

TOILETS

I hate car boot toilets. Antiques fairs have higher stall rent and entrance fees, plus longer days, so they have a vested interest in having decent facilities. Car boots don't. I will do absolutely anything to avoid using the toilets. Why? They're…

- Filthy
- Smelly
- Often unisex (more offensive to women than men, apparently)
- Doors don't always lock
- Long queues
- Just plain awful

Toilets at car boots are best avoided if at all possible – if the organiser has even supplied them.

I go to the toilet en route before I arrive at the car boot and then try not to drink anything (especially coffee because it is a diuretic) no matter how cold the start of the day. I do make an exception in hot weather when I drink water, but I try not to drink too much because I hate car boot toilets. So much so that, when I was filming *Boot Sale Challenge* and tried to wait until I had no choice, I saw the toilets being taken away before the event had even finished. Just go before you arrive and try to wait, if possible, until you have a more pleasant option. Also, it's worth noting that not all car boots actually have facilities, regardless of whether they should. I stalled at one event which usually had them but the supplier hadn't provided any that particular day. It caused huge problems, as you can imagine.

MONEY

Cash is the only acceptable method of payment, with one or two exceptions. They're firms which sell new (and often costly) garden furniture or brand-new three-piece suites. They are at the same venues most weeks and accept credit cards. Ask before buying and check that you have accurate contact details, just in case.

And it's not just cash you need but change. If you've haggled something down to £1.50 (or whatever), a £20 note will not be popular as the seller/buyer might not have enough change. Go prepared. You'll need a selection of the following:

- 5p

- 10p

- 20p

- 50p

- £1

- £5

You'll probably have £10 and £20 notes too. But don't expect to pay with a £50 note, because everyone is afraid of counterfeits – little realising that it's the lower value notes which get faked most. Not many car booters will accept Scottish £20 notes (unless they're in Scotland, of course) because of the amount of fakes around Not seeing them very often, people don't know what to spot so they tend to reject them just to be safe.

I try never to price anything with 5p at the end (e.g. £1.25, £9.75) because not everyone carries those tiny 5p coins with them. If selling, stick to rounder figures but always carry those 5ps with you for buying in case anyone haggles from £2 to £1.75. It really does happen!

Carrying change is probably the most important part of car booting. Just save up your coins for car boot days and take two or three purses with you as they are heavy. Also, you don't want to look too 'loaded' at car boots or your haggling appeal falters dismally. (Men, you can carry your coins in food bags if purses aren't your thing!) Rich people don't deserve discounts or shouldn't expect to get a high price. That's car boot logic. And I admit that I follow it. Why give an extra generous discount to someone whose diamond ring could probably buy my car?

As for notes, the £5 is always in short supply, so get extra from the bank before the event. They are also a useful tool in negotiating discounts, as many car booters never have enough of them and their own change runs out quickly – so someone able to pay with the 'right money' holds extra bargaining power.

HAGGLING

Haggling is more acceptable than it used to be. I even know people who get a discount at Marks & Spencers. And I never pay full price for any electrical goods I buy from large chain stores such as Currys. Haggling is a major part of life at car boots, so be prepared. As a seller, stick a tiny bit extra on the price of the goods to allow for bargaining – for example £6 for £5, £12 for £11, 90p for 60p. And yes, buyers will even haggle over 20p if you're unlucky! The offer of 'buy 12, pay for 10' is expected if you're selling cards, other cheaper items or a pile of CDs. As a seller, refusal to haggle will lose you sales as it's ingrained in the car booting culture, partly thanks to programmes like *Boot Sale Challenge* and *Car Booty*. BUT it's only on TV that you can ask for a

I bought this Thelwell ornament by Border Fine Art from Wimborne market. It was marked as £8; I paid £6 – and it's worth £50-60.

discount by offering a kiss in return. It's cringe-worthy but most female contributors thought they could get away with it. Please don't embarrass yourself or the seller by trying that on in real life. And it's not just women. Men have offered me a kiss in return for an extra large discount. Fortunately, I've never been that desperate! But let's be sensible. Haggling is part of car booting life but how do you do it?

As a buyer

If buying from an antique dealer at a car boot (though this advice also works at antiques fairs, shops, centres and second-hand bookshops), ask for the 'trade price' not the 'best price' as you'll generally get a bigger discount.

For other types of sellers, ask for the 'best price'. If buying several goods, stress this politely by asking: "If I'm buying all of these, what can you do?" (I'd actually add 'please' on the end, but that's me). The word 'if' introduces the idea that it had better be a good/realistic price or they'll lose the full sale.

SMILE – a friendly attitude translates into a better deal.

AS A SELLER

Okay, you're there to make money, but you also don't want to be stuck with stock/your belongings, so be flexible:

Stress that it's already cheap and add a 'but' to show willingness. SMILE so it's a friendly transaction.

Depending on the price, round down to the next level – 75p to 50p, £6 to £5, £50 to £45 – whatever feels right and you can get away with.

Then ask if they're looking for anything else. If you're a regular, tell them and suggest you can always see if you've got anything else of interest. Having said that, never buy anything especially for a buyer if it's too specialised, because you might never see them again.

Be realistic. Why are you car booting? To clear your belongings? To make money? If they're interested and the price is right, they'll buy it, but they might come back with a counter-offer. You can refuse, of course – but then offer another counter offer so they don't get caught up in Macho Rejection Syndrome and refuse to buy as they're not getting their own way. Keep smiling so it's a relaxed, friendly business, not just for them but for you. The day will pass faster that way too. If the price isn't right, thank them but say, 'I'm sorry, I just can't, it has to be £x', and then it's up to them. But be realistic about your price in the first place and think about whether you yourself would pay £x for it. If not, change your price or accept a lower offer.

Don't beat someone about the head asking for a discount. Think about what it's worth to you and let the sellers have their profit too. This Taunton Vale roller is worth £20-£25. I paid £5, accepting that the £1 discount was fair enough and still gave me more than a decent enough profit margin.

HOLDING ONTO PURCHASES

There will be times when either you need to leave your buys at a stall or, if a seller, are asked by a customer if they can do so. This is for practical reasons. Goods need packing, are too heavy to carry, you are meeting someone or because you are fetching or reparking a car. There's no reason not to, but just be practical:

What time is the seller leaving? Try to collect goods quickly so they don't disappear with them or have to wait for hours after they intended to leave.

Where is the seller stalling? Look for landmarks and exchange phone numbers if possible. Not all buyers and sellers will like this idea, so just make a note of the registration number and colour and type of car, plus row number/position.

Ask the seller if they'll help you to your car. This is generally fine later in the day but some might not be able to help when it's busy or if it's hard for them to carry the goods. However, most are accommodating where practical. If you don't live too far away, they may even offer to drop furniture or other large pieces at your home if your car is not big enough.

INTERESTED PARTIES

Car boots have changed so much in the last 10 to 15 years that they now attract a different type of seller. As a consequence, the police and Customs and Trading Standards officers are regular visitors to venues – as is the taxman. If someone at a car boot starts asking you questions and you have nothing to hide, request that they produce some form of ID. Never hand out your personal details to someone you don't know. Pirate DVD sellers are not as prolific as they were, thanks to these raids, but here are a few points to note if considering buying these illegal goods:

There are two types of pirate DVDs. One is filmed at the cinema and has people walking in front of the screen, coughing and fidgeting – but with no credits, as the camera had to be turned off as soon as possible to avoid detection. The quality tends to be variable, to say the least. The other type is a pirate copy with quality so variable that some don't even play. Other points to remember include:

- You don't often get a refund/swap if the DVDs don't work.
- You might not see the seller again.
- Your money (expect to pay around £2-5 for a pirate DVD) often finances criminal activities including drugs and human trafficking. A cheap DVD could be making someone else's life a misery.
- Trading Standards officers visit car boots to try to stop the pirate DVD trade.

LEAVING

Before leaving a car boot, ensure that your goods can't roll and get damaged. I know it's obvious, but so many people have complained about this happening over the years that it is worth stressing.

Not all car boots allow sellers to leave before a certain time. If not parked on the end of the row, it can be difficult to get out easily (but see p158 for tips on easier leaving) and there can be huge queues at the end of the event. As a seller, leave slightly early, but not too early, when the buyers have dried up. Pack quickly and leave to avoid the queues.

As a buyer, leave when you've had enough and collected all of your goods before everyone else, as queues and driving can be appalling. This applies especially at some of the larger venues such as Denham (see p170) where people drive up different rows to avoid the official queue and then cut in. If the main road is hard to cross because of sheer volume of traffic, drive the other way and turn round when convenient. It is often easier and safer that way.

Don't be a dummy. Enjoy your day out at the car boot and go prepared with plenty of change and carrier bags.

BUYING AT CAR BOOTS

Enjoy cut-price goods at car boots, including this stylish 1950s hairdresser's chair which was for sale at Brighton Station car boot.

CHAPTER 1

WHY BUY AT A CAR BOOT SALE?

THERE are many reasons to buy at a car boot, not just for bargains and saving and making money but also for very practical reasons, no matter what type of person you are. And let's start there. Just who buys from a car boot?

TYPES OF BUYERS

In the early days of car boots back in the 1980s and 1990s, they tended to appeal for purely financial reasons when people on low incomes were the main customers. Today, car boots encompass much wider markets. They attract families and anyone who wants:

You never know what you're going to find at a car boot. This one was at Longhill School, Rottingdean, where, apart from the plant stand, there were no professional dealers but plenty of parents selling their children's outgrown clothes, books and toys for a fraction of the price of new ones.

Decorate your home with bargains in the knowledge they are unique. It can be on the same budget as (or less than) flat-pack furniture but with a unique style that isn't as instantly recognisable as products from retailers such as Ikea.

- An enjoyable day out.
- To save money on otherwise costly toys and children's or baby's clothing.
- Cheap, market-type goods available with nearby parking.
- Cheap clothes and designer labels mixed with high street and catalogue clothing. Look carefully for amazing finds.
- Last year's fashion at affordable prices.
- Specialist dealers (see p45).
- Second-hand furniture.
- To find what can't be found elsewhere and at a good price.
- To add something to or find a missing item for their collection at a bargain price.
- Profits. Antique dealers look for stock with impressive profit margins as do vintage clothing and retro furniture sellers.
- Bargains from other people's unwanted belongings and other cheap goods.

DID YOU KNOW?

I wanted a fold-up table for work and when I was eating on my own. I looked in shops, at fairs and auctions but there wasn't anything suitable. They were either too expensive for what they were, too heavy, too small, too low or simply just not right. Then I went to a car boot and saw exactly what I wanted. I haggled, paid £3 and have used it virtually every day since. In fact, I'm writing this book on it right now, as well as four other books and I have written more than 3,000 articles on it and edited two different magazines. My bargain-priced table has been used in photo-shoots – and even occasionally for dining! It's not grand but it's exactly what I wanted. Shops were charging £20 to £30 for something which didn't even compare. That's a great saving.

I also wanted a plain, dark-coloured skirt in the days when everyone was selling loud patterns or frilly skirts in bright colours. I bought a Nicole Farhi heavy woollen skirt for a couple of quid. You would expect to pay £150-plus for something of that quality brand new.

WHAT TYPE OF PEOPLE SELL AT CAR BOOTS?

This is an interesting point and one of the reasons why car boots are now so popular. It's not just people selling off their belongings. Car boots now combine so many different elements – markets, antiques fairs and jumble sales, all the old way people disposed of their goods. Profits often went to charity in those days but today we live in a fashion-driven, commercial society where goods are replaced more often than previously and people want to get some of their money back, not just give it all away. Types of sellers include:

• Market traders: fruit and vegetables, electrical goods and accessories, stationery, food on the brink of going out of date, general market stalls (e.g. toilet paper), pet food and accessories, luggage, meat and fish etc.

Anyone can buy and sell at car boots – from people clearing their homes to professional dealers. The real mix of goods is one of the reasons so many people enjoy visits to car boots.

- Specialist dealers selling items such as records, second-hand CDs and DVDs (not just the odd few but tables full of them in a proper, legitimate business), outdoor good suppliers (e.g. tents and camping equipment), plant and flower suppliers (e.g. herbs, bedding plants, roses, cut flowers etc.), sporting good dealers (especially fishing reels), new and second-hand book dealers.
- Sellers of counterfeit goods: these are not as readily available as a few years ago but they still attract buyers, especially for pirate CDs and DVDs (see p36).
- Antique dealers. These can be general dealers, mixing china, glass and other goods, or specialist dealers selling items such as military, medals, coins and sporting goods.
- House clearancers. These often offer lower quality or damaged goods but there can be great bargains if you have a good rummage.
- Car boot dealers. These are not actually antique dealers but people who buy and sell specifically for the car boot market. This can range from clothes to china and glass. In fact, anything and everything.
- People selling their own belongings. This can often be where you get the best buys, although these sellers can overprice their goods and quality tends to vary. Personally, I wouldn't buy second-hand underwear from anyone.

WHY BUY AT CAR BOOTS?

It's for a number of reasons, ranging from bargains and potential profits to the mix of dealers and a fun day out. There are lots of sub-reasons within this but mainly it is all about being a sociable way of buying items for less than you'd expect to pay at most other venues. You can sell them on for a profit or just resell them when they've outlived their usefulness. I've bought loads of goods over the years, for myself, my home and for resale. I love the atmosphere, which is more relaxed than most antiques fairs these days as not everyone selling is trying to earn a living. The pitch fee is low so sellers don't have a large outgoing before they make a profit – meaning they won't be so tough when it comes to prices and haggling. And you really can make good money if you spot those bargain finds.

And what else is there to do at 7am on a sunny Sunday morning?

Fish for a bargain. Fishing tackle sellers are often regulars at car boots as low pitch rents make them the perfect 'plaice' to acquire cheap fishing accessories.

CHAPTER 2

FINDING THE RIGHT CAR BOOT SALE

THIS isn't just about flicking through the county-by-county directory at the back of this book (see p167), but about what you're looking for and your own lifestyle. I have a flexible workload so can do car boots mid-week and not just at weekends. It means I don't have to restrict where I go to buy. Not everyone can do that, of course. Some might choose to take the odd day off to go to their favourite car boots. Or, if it's their livelihood, others might do mid-week, as well as weekend car boots.

What do you want from a car boot? If looking for children's clothes, small local boots are ideal. You might need to travel to larger events if hoping to find specialist car booters such as this glass seller at Denham.

MID-WEEK CAR BOOTS

The mid-week ones have a very different feel to weekend car boots. They tend to be more dealer-led, which is also reflected in the buyers who are themselves dealers or collectors. There are fewer of the traditional car booters, such as people selling their own belongings, at mid-week venues because they're generally at work. So expect to see fewer children's clothes and toys but more collectables.

BANK HOLIDAY CAR BOOTS

Some of the best car boots are the irregular Bank Holiday ones, such as my favourite at the Rottingdean Cricket Club, Rottingdean, near Brighton in East Sussex (see p213 for details). Parking is a nightmare with queues blocking the road to and from Woodingdean but just arrive and leave early and get shopping. It's a real mix of sellers, with loads of them just normal people clearing their houses. It only takes place three times a year which means that, unlike some car boots, you won't see the same goods week after week and prices are competitive as people race to clear their goods. That is what's so good about the Bank Holiday events; people are effectively dumping their stuff ready for holidays, to get space or from spring or summer cleaning. There are dealers and specialist dealers but there are also great bargains. Look at some of these:

- Laura Ashley footstool: worth £75, paid £3.
- Quality, heavy, cream curtains: worth £60, paid £3.
- Books on tape: worth £9.99, paid £2.

Part of a Scandinavian decanter set I bought for 10p per piece. It's worth £50-60. The seller complained that I bought too much from them but at those prices they should have been asking what I knew that they didn't. This book will stop you from making the same mistake as those sellers.

These two glass and ceramic ashtrays by Purbeck Pottery were a fantastic find at Denham. They are by Robert Jefferson who once worked for Poole Pottery.

- Dog carrying cage: worth £25-30, paid £5.
- New hardback Jeffery Deaver bestseller: RRP £16, paid £2.
- Art Deco mirror: worth £75, paid £5.
- Scandinavian decanter set with six glasses: worth £50-60, paid 70p.
- 1950s Wade plate: worth £10, paid 10p.
- Victory wooden jigsaw with shapes: worth £15-20, paid 20p.

There are plenty of car boots at Bank Holiday time all over the country. Some of them are new events, so see your local press for details or look for roadside signs. Above all, take plenty of change for those must-buy bargains!

WHERE TO FIND CAR BOOTS

It depends what you're after but it's worth taking notice of what others have to report. If buying children's toys, speak to other parents at playgroups or at the school gates. Collectors and dealers should ask dealers or organisers at fairs, centres, auctions or shops. And don't forget to ask car booters to recommend other places. Do they stall elsewhere? If so, where? And what is it like? Word of mouth is better than any advertising but always check the local press and those hand-written road signs as new car boots spring up all the time. Also ask what is not worth doing because of bad facilities, awful parking, cars always getting bogged down etc. Be aware that not all dealers will want to share their car boot venues with you because competition when buying is bad for business. But they might be prepared to do so if they stall there as you could buy from them.

There are always fantastic finds at Ford, including Sammy Seal and Pluto, two Disney ornaments by Wadeheath. They were on sale for £60 each and at the time, worth £300 apiece.

AND FINALLY

Don't forget to check out the directory at the back of the book (see p167). I have my favourites and they're not always the biggest ones.

- Denham, Buckinghamshire, has one of the best car boots around and opens earlier than advertised. It's a really mixed event. I buy everything there from furniture for the home to some antiques and collectables with fantastic profit-margins, especially the tinplate toys (see p170).
- Ford boot fair in West Sussex is one of my favourites. It's on hard-standing so you can still go if it rains the night before. There are great collectables bargains from the professional dealers, house clearancers and those simply de-cluttering their homes (see p212).
- Wimborne, Dorset, used to be a fantastic antiques market but now combines car booting. It's not what it was back in the 1970s when I first started going but there are some great buys to be had from the combination of dealers and first-time sellers (see p181).
- The car boot at Shootash, Romsey, Hampshire, is a rambling venue and definitely worth a visit for the amount of quality collectables and interior design-led goods. There are also loads of children's toys on sale (see p189).
- Ashley Heath, on the Dorset-Hampshire border, has everything a good car boot should – collectables at incredibly good prices, quality clothes, children's 'must-haves' and everything for the home from good but cheap crockery to retro lighting and accessories. Just be careful about not getting caught in queues when you leave but it's worth it (see p180).
- Biggleswade used to be my local Bedfordshire car boot event and I was there every week. It is not worth travelling for as it's not huge but there are good buys, no matter what you're after (see p168).
- Rottingdean, East Sussex. The Bank Holiday event here is huge and a must-go car boot. See if nearby Peacehaven has an event on at The Dell as their fortnightly sale has very good buys. You can pay 10p+ for collectables so there could be a huge profit margin but it is not really worth the journey unless you're local or fancy a day out. I love it as it's great for kids' goods and household items, as well as collectables galore (see p213).

- Brighton Market up at the station isn't meant to be a car boot but is. The cars are parked by the stalls and there is a good mix of items on sale. At the time of writing, its future is uncertain. I've also bought some good but cheap fruit and vegetables alongside my jazz CDs and records, interior design accessories, cheap books and collectables with the Art Deco–1950s period being particularly well represented (see p212).

There is a very South-East bias here because that's where I've lived, worked and filmed but obviously there are good car boots all over the country. Just ask other collectors, dealers and keen car booters so you don't miss out on potential profit and bargain buys.

I love Brighton Station car boot but you do need to watch out for fakes. Apart from a few of those, the sellers are very friendly and there are bargains a-plenty in this central location but it might not be around for much longer.

CHAPTER 3

PREPARATION

IF YOU are thinking of going to a local car boot, be brave and just turn up – unless it's pouring with rain when few sellers are likely to be around. If you have to travel and the weather hasn't been wonderful, ring the organisers before setting out. I've turned up to film at car boots which were cancelled the day before because of rain, even when the weather was forecast as fine on the day of the car boot itself. I know it might seem odd travelling for a car boot if you haven't done so before but some, such as Denham, really are worth it. If you are lucky, what you pay for in petrol will be more than made up in profits. Combine a visit with lunch out, make a day of it or go to antiques fairs and other car boots in the area.

DON'T FORGET

There are basic items you need to take to every car boot, regardless of what you're buying (see also p30). These are:

- Blankets or cloths for hiding buys and wrapping items such as polished and antique furniture or paintings to prevent them from getting scratched.
- Food and drink. Save time and money by taking your own. Avoid salty fry-ups unless you really, really want them. Don't forget to take a flask of hot tea or coffee, as the early starts can be surprisingly cold even if the forecast is for a heatwave later in the day.
- Bags. Take loads of them as not all sellers will provide them. (Or you might be palmed off with bags with holes or ones that break easily.) Recycle supermarket bags while we still have them, as they are surprisingly strong and roomy. I also take a couple of bags I can carry over my shoulder to keep my hands free.
- Wrapping. Some sellers might not have enough wrapping

materials – or any at all. So take newspaper with you and bubble-wrap if you're buying very fragile goods. It's not just that sellers might not have enough wrapping paper, but also what they offer can be scrappy, holey or smell of stale cigarette smoke.

- Boxes or extra large bags. Keep these in the car to stop everything rolling around as you drive home. We are not just talking about breakables but plants, toy cars and anything else which might tip over or move when travelling.

- Change and £5 notes. Get bags of coins from the bank ready for the car boot and put them in different purses/wallets/bags. That way, you don't show just how much you're carrying, as this isn't a great idea when you are trying to get extra discounts. Even £10 notes might be difficult for some sellers to change, so take plenty of £5 notes and £1 and 50p coins in particular. (see p32)

- A map. Plot your route before setting off. If you don't know exactly where you're travelling, you must be beady-eyed when driving to the venue – not just as the entrance might not be where expected but you might spot signs to other car boots along the way.

- Mobile phone. Not everyone carries them at the weekend when they want to shut down from work, but you'll need one in case you break down or in case you need to ring a partner, friend or helpful dealer for advice about something that has caught your eye.

- *Car Boot and Fairs Calendar*. Open to the car boot listings to see what else is on that day (see p221 for details). Or just take this book with you and use the directory (see p167).

- Calculator. This might sound silly but it is still worth thinking about as not everyone can add up, especially when buying in odd units such as 20p and 70p. It just means you don't pay more than you should.

- Be prepared for the weather. You'll need extra water, sun hat, sunglasses and suntan lotion in the summer and plastic coat and perhaps wellies for rainy days. Umbrellas can be taken but they'd probably get in the way.

- Check your coat or jacket before you go. If it's at the right height to knock goods off the stalls, either change or just be extra careful, especially when reaching over. I've seen a lot of costly accidents over the years at car boots and antiques fairs, so it's something to think about.

- Price guides. Some collectors take these to car boots. That's fine if you have to, but leave them in the car and never let the seller know what you know or suspect about what you're buying or the price will go up.

Go prepared. Take plenty of bags, food and drink with you and wear lots of layers, as it often starts out cold and can then warm up – or even rain!

CHAPTER 4

WHAT TO BUY

I AM NOT claiming to give a definitive list here or this book would be too heavy to lift! Instead, I am giving examples of what you might expect to buy at car boots, particularly with profits and savings in mind. I won most of my rounds on *Boot Sale Challenge* because I could advise my contributors on what to buy – and it wasn't always what was obviously worth money.

My background is antiques fairs. I've bought a lot from auctions over the years, as well as acted as a consultant to what's now Bonhams in London's New Bond Street and worked on several antiques programmes, including *Name Your Price*, Everything Must Go and *Under the Hammer*. But my fellow experts were always auctioneers and, although great at their jobs, their scope was more limited because of that. Not for them Avon cats in their original boxes (bought for £1, worth £15-25) or empty tin boxes for Border Fine Art collectables (bought for 20p, worth £5) but more serious items with smaller profit margins. That's why I won so often. I understand car boot buys, not just auction values. And that's what I'm going to share with you here – the secret of how to maximise your profits or just save loads of money.

The reality is that some of you know exactly what you are hoping to find; you're collectors, are looking for specific goods for your house, or maybe you're just browsing idly. But still read on. There is money to be made and money to be saved. Even if you go out to buy one thing, who knows what will be in your car by the end of the sale?

WHAT TO BUY FOR SAVINGS AND PROFITS

The following all depends on the item being of good or usable quality. Collectors might want their vintage Dinky toy vehicles MIB (mint in boxes) but two or three-year-olds just want something they can play with. So a 50p car is worth far more than that to them than to a collector who is looking for excellent condition unless the item is particularly rare.

Toys

You might want toys for your kids without paying shop prices in the knowledge they'll get bored with them so quickly. Car boots are perfect for this. Just check that the games are complete and don't have chew marks! But if buying for a profit, your needs are different. Or are they? What

This 1969 Corgi Ford Mustang 'Flower Power' car is worth £500-800 MIB because so few were produced. So it's worth rummaging around boxes of old toys. This one cost 50p at a car boot but, even allowing for its condition, it's still worth £80-120.

some people do is buy modern games, including jigsaws, at car boots and sell them for a profit to other parents on eBay.

Then there are collectable toys. This is what I love doing. Rummage around people's boxes, because collectable toys get thrown out when people decide to empty their lofts, sheds or garages or they want to move. At this point, out come the 1950s-plus toys. And that's where the money is. Most people can spot the old TV favourites but do they know what they're worth? Vintage *Magic Roundabout* is often quite valuable, whilst the modern one isn't. (Dougal's nose looks too large and cheap in modern versions and his eyes are too 'human'.) The Corgi Carousel of the *Magic Roundabout* in its original box sells for £300-500 and can still be found at a boot fair.

Old wooden jigsaws – especially the old Victory ones and those with shapes such as animals hidden within the image (not children's farmyard ones) – sell for around £2 to £6 at car boots but you can get around £20-plus for them at fairs or on eBay.

A 1973 Matchbox bus with a sign for Carnaby Street, the popular fashion-led street of the time. This period detail should instantly grab your attention. Buy for 50p and sell, in this condition, for £8-12 on eBay.

Don't forget to look at dolls – old Sindys, Barbies, Action Men and their accessories, including 1960s Sindy dresses designed by Sally Tuffin. These can be worth a lot of money but there is little knowledge in this area so most dealers wouldn't know what to spot. See Susan Brewer's *British Dolls of the 1960s* for details, and also her *British Dolls of the 1950s*, both published by Remember When in 2009.

CHILDREN'S BOOKS

Great for kids but also for profit, this is an area that dealers often overlook as they don't always know what to seek out. A first edition Enid Blyton Famous Five mystery can fetch £300-500 but how many people think of checking? Take your time and make a profit. Sell them on eBay, Amazon or Abe Books (www.abebooks.co.uk). Rarer ones, such as a first edition of early books by top authors (see p128) or signed books are worth taking to a specialist auction sale such as Bloomsbury Auctions (020 7495 9494 or www.bloomsburyauctions.com).

Whilst many dealers realise that some Observer books are worth more than the 50p-£1 charged, they don't necessarily know which ones to buy. And they might not even think of buying Ladybird books. Do your research for maximum profits.

Adults' books

I buy a lot of books at car boots because I read three or four a week, as well as wanting to make a profit. Expect to pay 20p-50p for modern paperbacks (some cost up to £1) and 50p-£2 for hardbacks. Look for first-edition early crime books of best-selling authors (see p128) for surprisingly large profits. Again, don't forget to look for signed copies. Sell them on eBay, Amazon or Abe Books (www.abebooks.co.uk) or via an auction house such as Bloomsbury Auctions (see the previous page for details).

Magazines and ephemera

Some old magazines are just very interesting but others can be worth money. Ephemera, including old diaries and letters, can also be valuable but it's a specialist area overlooked by many general dealers at car boots – and that's what can make bargains easy to find. Dealers often don't know what they're selling, so it can be worth buying a bundle after a quick flick through and doing your research afterwards.

Ephemera. Here today, gone tomorrow – unless you know what to look out for.

CHILDREN'S CLOTHES

Save money by buying your fast-outgrown kids' clothes at car boots. Or buy 'designer' brands such as Gap for 50p-£2 at the car boots and sell them for more on eBay. Don't forget to check for stains and damage before buying, as well as missing buttons and broken zips.

ADULT CLOTHING

There are bargains galore to be had at boot sales, not just by buying clothes to wear but to sell on. Look for designer names such as Calvin Klein, Vivienne Westwood, Christian Dior, Nicole Farhi and Jaeger. I bought a £150 Jaeger jacket for £3 and, even allowing for the dry cleaning costs, it was still an absolute bargain. Just sell on to a dress agency or via eBay, taking into account any costs to make them saleable. Check that the buttons are all there and that there are no stains under the arms or anywhere else.

Vintage clothes are great bargains as people empty out their closets. Look for Biba and Pucci but also Laura Ashley and clothes evocative of their era. Sell them on eBay under the 'retro' or 'vintage' banner for maximum profit.

Look for designer names and vintage clothing at car boots. Or just treat yourself to a bargain buy.

Shoes

Second-hand shoes might not sound appealing. But many women wear new shoes for just for one season, or find they pinch so sell them on after just one wear. Look at the soles for wear and tear, check that the lining is intact and that they're definitely a pair and not two left feet! Then sell them on eBay. Turn a £2 buy into a £20-£30 designer footwear profit.

Handbags

Look for torn linings and broken zips, as well as designer labels. Handbags cost around 50p-£2 at boot sales and from £15 upwards on eBay. I bought an American, Enid Collins bag with poodle decoration for around £3 and sold it for £90 on eBay. As with anything sequinned or beaded, check for fraying before buying, as they can be difficult, or impossible, to repair.

Costume Jewellery

Costume jewellery is often overlooked by dealers because they assume anything 'fake' isn't worth buying. But a set of Miriam Haskell pearls can be worth the same or even more than a set of genuine pearls. Other names to spot include:
- Chanel
- Schiaparelli
- Joseff, who designed 90% of the jewellery in 1930s-40s Hollywood, as well as a retail range. His work has a distinctive 'old gold' colouring
- Nettie Rosenstein
- Hattie Carnegie, especially her African series with its two-coloured animal brooches and bangles
- Coro. Look for Coro Duettes with the double brooches on a single clasp
- Eisenberg, especially her 'Ice' series of fake diamonds
- Christian Dior. Look for signatures including Mitchel Maer
- Ken Lane, especially the earlier pieces which are signed KJL

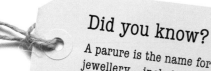

Did you know?

A parure is the name for a set of jewellery, including necklace, earrings and bracelet.

REAL JEWELLERY

Not every seller knows what he or she has got, and you could spend under £1 on something worth hundreds. Take the time to look through boxes of jewellery. Check for hallmarks and signatures. But don't ever bring out a hallmark book in front of the seller or you'll alert them to a potential mistake and they'll withdraw the goods or up the price. Keep quiet for maximum profits. Remember that rings can be resized (check if the band is worn as it could snap if the metal is too thin), stones recast and diamonds re-polished. All this cuts into your profit margins but knowing what is possible could save you from turning down a real bargain.

GOLD AND SILVER

You'll find many dealers selling gold and silver at car boots. They are the ones with jewellery cases – but this doesn't mean they know everything about the subject, so see what they've got. Attractive boxes

A combination of silver and silver jewellery from a professional dealer at less than the cost of a high street shop.

sell but vestas (matchboxes) and cigarette cases have become harder to sell because of today's attitude towards smoking. I used to sell them with ease but struggle these days unless the cases can hold business cards. Don't forget also to look at general stalls for hidden profits. And a final word of warning: don't take anyone's word that they're selling silver and gold; I still see EPNS (silver plate) being sold on as genuine silver, not through dishonesty but ignorance.

MEDALS

People sell their family possessions through car boots, often not realising the value of what they have. And because they feel intimidated by auctions, they miss out on expert advice. Take the time to look through medals, not just war medals but ones honouring sporting achievements as well. One lucky car booter paid £10 for a medal celebrating Manchester United's Championship League success in the 1996-97 season. He sold it at auction for £6,400. Even after his commission had been deducted, that's a huge profit – and the reason why so many of us go to car boots.

MUSIC

With CDs having dominated the music scene, many buyers don't even look at records – but there's money to be made if you do. Buy a price guide (one of the few accurate price guides in the antiques and

Buy cheap CDs at car boots and sell them for a profit on eBay or Amazon.

Save a fortune by buying your children's instruments from car boots.

collectables field, in my opinion) and start learning what's worth buying. Don't overlook CDs, not just for personal enjoyment but because you can buy them at 50p £2 and sell them for a profit on eBay or Amazon.

INSTRUMENTS

Not the most obvious place for a musical instrument but don't let your kids miss out on practising. Buy bargain instruments at car boots when other children have grown bored of their hobby.

SPORT

Find cheap balls, bats and other sporting accessories at car boots. Fishing tackle is a great buy as the seller doesn't have the overheads of a shop. Old balls and bats can also be worth money to the right market. Some golf clubs and even balls can make thousands. Do your research and sell those fantastic finds at specialist sporting auctions.

Reel in a bargain with car boot-bought fishing tackle.

It might look a pile of rust but some tools are both useful and collectable. Look carefully, so you don't miss out on potential profits.

TOOLS

Judging by how many are sold at car boots, tools are very good buys. Whilst some modern tools are not built to last, the old ones were. Either buy for use or look for vintage tools to sell on. Spot signed planes and lathes and other collectable tools and sell them at specialist sales.

KITCHENALIA

People wanting to upgrade or clear out cupboards virtually give away vintage kitchenalia, not realising it has a strong market. Look for T. G. Green's blue and white crockery, old mixing bowls and other collectable goods. Sell them on eBay but beware of postage costs. The best option to avoid having heavy, costly goods to post would be to save up a few boxfuls, then stall out at an antiques fair. Also look for crockery by the likes of Denby and Midwinter which were very popular in the 1950s and 1960s, with many of today's buyers wanting replacement goods for their original sets. But as they are heavy to post, take them to antiques fairs for maximum profits.

Celebrity chefs, food magazines and vintage style have brought kitchenalia back into fashion for its practical usage as well as good looks, including these cake, sorbet and chocolate moulds.

China

One of the biggest areas of collectables is also the most commonly faked (see p74) but there are plenty of bargains to be had at car boots. Some of the best opportunities are from dealers who use car boots to sell old stock at great prices to get their money back or break even. Check everything carefully for damage and restoration work. (It will feel different to the rest of the piece – rougher or smoother – and the balance could be uneven). Dinner, tea and coffee services are fantastic buys for use but generally not for resale. The market in these is not what it was, with the exception of top quality makes such as Susie Cooper, Clarice Cliff and Burleigh. Animal ornaments are always popular, as are stylish, signed pieces (unsigned goods are harder to sell). Makes to look out for if going for top collectability include:

- Beswick: Stick to the animals – not the vases – especially licensed goods such as Beatrix Potter.
- Blue and white. Not a make but a very collectable style.
- Burleigh: Crockery with distinctive hand-painted edging.
- Carlton Ware: Blush (peach-coloured) and jewel-like decorated pieces do well but you're more likely to find their novelty goods such as Walking Ware at car boots.
- Charlotte Rhead: Art Deco, tubular designs.
- Clarice Cliff: Brilliantly coloured Art Deco pieces. Don't buy the monotone, wartime pieces.
- Denby: Try to find their figural pieces which aren't always signed but have a trademark, chalky glaze or a brilliantly sharp electric blue glaze.
- Fiesta Ware: Shapely American, monotone, practical pieces (see p70).

- George Jones and other Majolica ware: Salt-glazed rich turquoise and green-based decorative wares.
- Goebel: Humorous German pottery with a V backstamp with a bee over it.
- Goldscheider: Flowing Art Deco German figures.
- Midwinter: Animals with distinctive eyes, even though they're not all signed, plus sellable crockery.
- Paragon: Delicate porcelain tea and coffee services.
- Poole Pottery: Brightly-coloured studio ware from the 1960s or earlier, tile-heavy figures. Later figures don't have the same type of market so stick to ones with embossed backstamps and not printed ones.
- Toni Raymond: My tip for what will be the next big collectable. Look for its distinctive kitchenalia but also try to find animals which few people know Raymond made, including a signed polar bear.
- Royal Copenhagen: Look for its studio ware and animals.
- Royal Crown Derby: Garishly-coloured, highly collectable. Blue, gold, red and white crockery, including figures.
- Royal Doulton: Figures – not crockery – are the best buys or any licensed goods, including Brambly Hedge and The Snowman.
- Royal Worcester: Delicate figures or candle-snuffers.
- Staffordshire: Collectable clumpy Victorian classic ornaments and fireside friends.
- Susie Cooper: Shapely Deco and 1950s crockery.
- Wade: Not what it was in terms of money but there's still a market for the animals, Disney pieces and Deco figures.
- Wedgwood: Jasper Ware is its most popular style, especially if selling on eBay to an international market.

Carlton Ware Coronation Street mug, questionable Poole Pottery dolphins (moulding crude as they're fake) and fake, overly-light and colourful Staffordshire dogs based on Queen Victoria's spaniel, Dash.

Practical pottery such as this American-made Fiesta Ware jug are good buys at car boots. I paid £3 for this and it's worth £30-£50. I'll sell it on eBay where it will attract American interest.

GLASS

This is a good area to get into because lack of general knowledge, including dealers, allows for bargain finds. Not all glass is signed (which is one of the reasons it has never been as popular as china) but learn to spot styles. Avoid the garish Murano clowns which are impossible to date as they've been made the same way for so long. Watch out for other makes including:

- Baccarat: Signed with a logo of glasses and its name.
- Carnival glass: Ready for its 15-year revival so buy now to profit when it comes back in fashion within the next couple of years.
- Daum: French Art Nouveau (pronounced Dome).
- Davidson: Look for its practical cloud glass pieces such as vases.
- Gallé: French Art Nouveau.
- Holmegaard: Chunky Scandinavian glass.
- Lalique: Classic French Art Deco glass. The best pieces are signed; later pieces have a printed signature. Buy anything you can if the price is right.
- Loetz: Best known for its pearl glass.
- Carlo Moretti: Stylish figural glass.
- Orrefors: Signed on the bottom in a hard-to-read script.
- Pressed glass. Not a make but a style.
- Salviati: The best glassmaker to come out of Murano, in my opinion.
- Stourbridge: Makers include Thomas Webb and Stevens and Williams. Look for the rose-pink tones and soft Victorian colours as well as stylish designs.
- Sowerby: Including slag glass, a style with deep colours sometimes mixed with white.

- Tiffany: Famed for his lamps using his 'favrille' (handmade) glass.
- Vaseline glass: Named after its thick and yellowy colour.
- Waterford: Irish crystal signed with a seahorse logo and its name.
- Whitefriars: The daytime TV antiques show favourite. Stick to the jewel-like colours for best buys.

ART DECO

The distinctive shapely goods from the Art Deco period (1925-39) are surprisingly cheap car boot finds, especially the chrome pieces.

This Art Deco chrome tea-strainer was a fantastic buy for £2.50 at Denham car boot. It's worth £15-25.

Art

Don't overlook paintings at car boots. Beneath the tat are treasures. One example was an 1869 portrait of Crimean nurse Mary Secole, bought at a car boot by a dealer who didn't recognise the sitter and resold it at auction. It is now on loan to the National Portrait Gallery. If the buyer had done his research first, he would have made an even bigger profit.

Did you know?

A buyer wanted a piece of blue and white by the little known Limehouse pottery but saw that it was damaged and asked for a 50 per cent discount. She paid 50p for the sauceboat, which sold later for an amazing £9,400. It was one of the earliest pieces of British porcelain, dating to around 1790 when blue and white porcelain was first created in Britain.

CHAPTER 5

WHAT NOT TO BUY

NOT EVERYTHING sold at car boots is legal. Either it's counterfeit (e.g. pirate DVDs) or it's on sale illegally (e.g. certain weapons). In both cases, the seller is generally knowingly breaking the law. Legal guidelines, however, are a bit hazy when it comes to what exactly is illegal to buy. My advice is that if it's illegal to sell, then for your own sake don't buy it. In some cases, such as BB air guns, the danger is that not everyone will realise they are not real. They're often sold at a car boot near me, and children have been injured playing with them. There are also goods which are not worth buying for Health and Safety reasons or because they just might not work and you could be wasting your money. Oh, and don't trust the person who says it does work. They won't be there tomorrow or even next week when you try to get your money back.

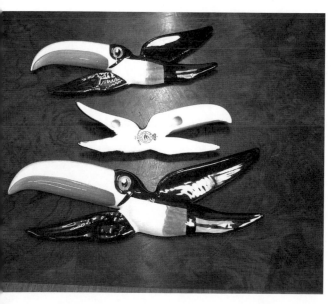

Fakes are common at car boots. Look for overly-bright colours and bad backstamps. Original pieces will have a script signature, unlike this one, and the weight will feel too light and unbalanced. Once you learn genuine markings, you won't get caught out.

WHAT NOT TO BUY

- Pirate DVDs and CDs. Apart from the legality and ethics, there's no guarantee that they'll work and the quality is variable. You might not be able to hear or see the film properly and it could die halfway through. They're simply not worth the money.
- Guns.
- BB guns which are easily mistaken for real guns and can cause injuries.
- Knives as weapons (not cutlery) and swords.
- Electrical goods, such as DVD players and TVs unless you can see that they work. Some dealers will have a generator hooked up or another way to show that their TVs etc. work. Don't buy anything unless you know you're not wasting your money. Remember, with few exceptions, you won't be offered a guarantee, even for new appliances.
- Baby's and children's car seats. I wouldn't advise anyone to buy a second-hand car seat, no matter whether it's at a car boot sale or a second-hand shop. The seller might not be aware of any flaws, such as less obvious wear and tear which could place your child at risk. Health and Safety laws have changed, so some 'nearly new' seats breach current regulations. It's not worth it.
- Aluminium kitchenware such as saucepans which are no longer believed to be safe because they are carcinogenic.
- Cracked crockery for use as it can harbour bacteria and make you ill.
- Collectables such as Homemaker china which is the wrong weight and where the backstamp is either blurred or just doesn't look right. Beware, there are a lot of fakes at car boots.
- Wade NatWest pig money-boxes whose colours are too bright and the edges too sharp as these are often faked. They're probably the most common fake collectables to find at car boots.
- Carlton Ware Guinness collectables with clumsy mouldings and bright colours; also Carlton tortoise cruets or cruise liners. These are all fakes.
- Soft furnishings such as sofas without the requisite fire safety labels. These are unsafe to use as they're not fire retardant.

Carlton Ware never made these liners with Carlton backstamps. They are fakes, but only experience – and this book – will tell you that. They also didn't make tanks, tortoise cruets, golf player ornaments or Hitler ornaments.

Car boot tips

A student recently paid an astonishing £600 for a TV set spotted at a car boot sale. The seller then took it away to put in its box. Unfortunately, the box contained a load of potatoes instead. I wouldn't pay £600 for anything at a car boot where I don't know who the seller is and when no warranty is offered. This sorry transaction was much publicised. But a few weeks later another person got caught out over the purchase of a £400 laptop in a box – only to discover that the box was actually stuffed with phone directories. Make sure you look in the box before handing over your hard-earned cash.

Don't buy anything, especially electrics, and then turn your back. Have you ever wondered if a lorry has lost a load recently? That said, I bought a DVD player in its original box for £20 from a seller who was there every week and gave me his phone number (which I checked actually existed before handing over my cash). He sold electrical goods for a living and had legitimate excess stock he wanted to clear.

CHAPTER 6

BUYING TIPS AND HAGGLING

BOOT sales are fun and they're like no other business. Go to a souk in the Middle East and you'll be expected to haggle because it's part of the culture. Car boot sales are not the same. For many of the sellers, it is not their main livelihood but haggling is still part of the currency. However, before you start haggling, let's get buying.

I've already suggested some of the items you might wish to buy if you don't have specific ideas in mind already, but there's more to it than just finding the goods.

WHERE TO START

Unless I'm there to see a particular seller or have a favourite stall I like to go to first, I always go round car boots systematically, down one side of the aisle and up the other, not crossing over (unless the stalls are clearly not of interest to me e.g. auto parts or lawnmowers), but thoroughly. It's not like antiques fairs where you can see virtually at a glance if the stalls are of interest. Car boots are so much more general that a stall seemingly full of children's clothes might have another box underneath containing bargain finds. Just take your time – although don't be too slow or you could miss out on some great finds.

Rummage around to find hidden treasures.

Prices

Not everyone prices their goods, especially the house clearancers who have boxes of items and those selling their own goods. To be honest, most make it up as they go along. Some might have boxes or areas marked 'all for 50p' or suchlike and others might just say 'everything 10p'. Dealers and market traders tend to price their stock or have labels marking the prices of the goods in certain areas or types of goods (e.g. CDs £3, DVDs £4). People selling books tend to mark the prices in pencil inside the front cover or on the boxes in which they're being sold.

That's the easy part. Others set their prices by how much they think they can get away with. I've heard one seller up his price by £2 when a better-dressed person asked the price. And that's where you start – with what to wear.

Dressing down

I start with a dressing down! No designer goods, no smart shoes, absolutely no jewellery. Having said which, obviously wedding rings are fine, although you might want to twist pricey engagement rings round for the duration of the sale. A £3,000 diamond will not get you great discounts and prices could go up as soon as the canny seller spots it. Dress not to impress, and you can always get changed later if intending to eat out. Just layer up and remove the less smart top layer. But what should you wear for best prices and great deals?

Sensible shoes. Men, I'm not really aiming this at you but don't wear your best brogues. Apart from anything else, most car boots take place in fields. So don't wear stilettos or suede shoes – you could get stuck or they may get ruined. If it's been raining heavily, take wellies or trainers which can be put in the washing machine when you get home. I tend to take boots with me and remove them when I get to the car, storing them in a plastic bag brought along for the purpose, so my boot doesn't get muddy. I do the same when I'm attending antiques fairs at showgrounds when it's been wet.

Tops. Again, nothing designer but be practical. It's cold first thing when you arrive and will hopefully warm up later, so put on layers. A big jumper could leave you sweltering and a vest top will be too cold first thing. If you intend to go somewhere nice afterwards, keep your smart top under the boot sale-friendly one for best buys.

Jackets or coats. These can be removed and left in the car as it gets warmer. Just be careful that a waist-length jacket doesn't knock goods off tables.

Trousers or skirts. Again, think of the weather. You don't want good trousers or long skirts getting muddy. Jeans are best as you can also keep change in your pocket.

Jewellery. Be sensible. I'm not thinking security but discounts. Someone covered in expensive jewellery is not going to get discounts, as they can clearly afford the goods on offer. And, if buying jewellery, the seller (especially a general dealer or someone clearing a house) is going to assume that what they have is actually really good quality – even if they bought it from cheaper retailers such as H. Samuels or Argos. Prices will rise and haggling won't be nearly as successful as would be the case with someone who doesn't wear anything apart from a wedding ring.

Hats. If you're susceptible to sunstroke, wear a hat at car boots as the sun may be stronger than you expect, especially if you are wandering around for a couple of hours. I speak from experience here as I always underrate both the sun's strength and how long I'll be at the car boot.

Give sellers space if you want them to give you a better deal and never unpack their car or boxes for them unless you ask first.

How to get the best deals

Okay, so you're suitably dressed, but what else should you do? Well, the best thing to wear is a smile – and it won't cost you a thing! It really does work. Asking for advice or a discount in a friendly manner with a smile encourages people to want to help. Glare or demand a better price and they won't be quite so helpful. I like people, so it's easy for me to engage them, get any extra information if I need it and end up with a good deal. As a seller, it's amazing just how rude people can be when they actually want a favour.

Give sellers space. I've had people try to open my car doors and boot and take things out to look at them as soon as I arrive. That's not how to get someone on side. Let the sellers take their boxes out and ask, politely, if it's okay to rummage. They'll generally agree and carry on emptying their car or sorting out other boxes.

Have the bottle to haggle – but do it nicely for maximum profit. Aggression can incur an instant 'no', so smile, be polite and get a bigger discount.

Don't hang back too far or you could lose the chance to buy. If a seller is unpacking, just call across to ask them the price of what you've seen. They are there to sell so will be pleased to help.

Be friendly when asking for the price and add the word 'please'. Not 'how much?' but 'how much is this, please?' Trust me, a little politeness can save you money.

If they don't have quite what you want but there's similar on their pitch, inquire further – ask for exactly what you want or if they have anything else similar. Chances are that there's either another box lurking in the car or that they can get someone to bring it from home

CAR BOOT TIPS

I met a seller at her first – and last – boot sale. Obviously an amateur, the well-dressed woman was descended on by the dealers, who took things out of her car and didn't ask before rummaging. I did. She told the others to get lost and I had first look at some wonderful pieces of china and jewellery. She just wanted to sell, had an upsetting start and her prices reflected this. I did very well, all because I was polite and asked first.

on this occasion or next time if they're not local.

Ask questions – nothing too probing, like exactly where they live, but something friendly; perhaps a gentle question about their kids, if buying children's toys or clothes. However, never ask about pets if a dog bed, hamster cage or suchlike is for sale, as there might be a very sad reason why they're selling it.

If you want several items from a stall, make a pile or store everything in one place right by you. Otherwise someone else could reach over and buy the goods, not realising that you're interested. Don't just assume the seller will say it's yours if you haven't agreed a price; no one wants to lose a firm, alternative sale if money hasn't been agreed. You can always tell sellers that you definitely want the goods and ask them to put them behind the stall as you continue looking.

HAGGLING

Haggling is expected (See also p154). You can pay the full price if you want to (especially on really cheap goods such as 10p items) but why not try to get a better deal? Actually, I never ask for discounts on even a stack of 10p goods. They're just 10p after all and I know that they're worth a lot more than that. However, if buying several items, most sellers will offer a discount automatically. If not, ask. But how far can you go?

This is often based on what they're charging and what it is actually worth. I haggle for most goods (over 10p, that is). If you don't, they suspect they may be selling too cheaply. It doesn't help that I've done a few antiques shows and my face is on the cover of *Car Boot Calendar*, so I get recognised occasionally. But people are friendly and like discussing my articles and the antiques trade in general so I don't get overcharged.

If you know something is worth considerably more than what you're paying, be generous. Ask for a discount but not a huge one to allow the seller to make money.

There are two ways to get discounts – offer an exact sum (for a £12 item, 'Will you take £10?') or ask what they'll take ('What's the best price, please?'). As I said before, if they're a dealer, ask for the 'trade price' for a bigger discount. My dad had been a dealer for over 30 years when he decided to take my advice and ask about the trade price instead of offering a certain sum. He ended up saving an extra £5. This is certainly the best advice at antiques fairs and also works at car boots.

To be honest, it depends on the seller. Some will try to get more if you ask for a better price, whereas offering a set price makes it look like you've determined on the maximum amount you're prepared to pay. In some cases, this is true and I've refused to pay the discounted price for some goods (garden and household, not collectables) because the sellers (not dealers) were not realistic about what they were charging. I knew what the items were worth and wouldn't pay over the odds – and nor should you. Know what you're prepared to pay and if the profit margin isn't high, just let it go if they won't agree to a reasonable offer.

But, as a last resort, check if the item you're after is still there before you leave. After all, a couple of hours on, the sellers might be more realistic about their expectations.

Always check that you're not buying a fake. This cranberry oil lamp just isn't right. The moulding is too crude on both the glass and base and the lampshade is too heavy-looking. The Staffordshire spaniels on the left are also fakes, as their coarse moulding and poor colouring show.

CHAPTER 7

GENERAL ADVICE AND WARNINGS

DEPENDING what you're buying, there are certain things you need to check before making purchases at car boots. If buying electrical goods, check the plugs before using them, tighten or re-insert wires if necessary, and have a spare fuse ready, just in case.

BUYING COLLECTABLE CHINA AND GLASS

This is standard advice but not everyone thinks to check when buying at car boots – especially if not wanting to show that they've found something worth money or if the goods are particularly grubby. This is particularly true of house clearance lots and dusty items from people's garages and lofts. Not everyone cleans the goods before selling them, especially if a little dust hides a little crack...

You need to check the following:

- Is it perfect? Look for chips and cracks, as well as restoration. If it's rare, it might still be worth buying if the damage is minimal and the price is right.
- Is the backstamp right or is the piece of china too light or heavy? If in doubt, don't waste your money, because you can't sell fakes on without harming your own reputation. If you unwittingly buy any, fakes are best smashed to avoid others getting caught out.
- Look at the moulding and colouring. Boot sales are fantastic places to offload fakes and the price isn't always a giveaway. I've seen so many and they're easy to spot when you're used to them. Most people are so excited to find such 'bargains' or 'reasonably priced' goods at venues renowned for good prices, that they don't think to check whether they're real, repro or just plain fake.
- If buying figures or animals, don't forget to check that the legs, arms, heads, feet, fingers or tails have not been stuck back on.

Does your clock tick and keep time? Ask the dealer to wind it up and wait for a few minutes to see the hands turn. If it's an absolute bargain, snap it up before someone else does. Always ask if clocks have keys before buying them.

- If the goods are marked by labels and not backstamps, check that the labels are accurate. Does it actually look like Beswick, Sylvac etc. or has someone added a good make to a bad piece or fake?

FAKES TO EXPECT

I always see the same old fakes making the rounds and you probably do as well, even if you don't necessarily realise it. Be very careful if you're buying any of the following:
- Clarice Cliff – backstamp crude and smudged, moulds clumsy, colours too bright).
- Sylvac rabbits and Terrier – backstamp crude and smudged, moulds clumsy, colours too bright, also sometimes have stuck-on labels declaring them to be Sylvac, when they're not.
- Wade NatWest pigs – moulds clumsy, colours too bright.

- Carlton Ware Guinness figures, tortoise cruets, tank and cruise liner – backstamp crude and smudged, moulds clumsy, colours too bright (see p75).
- Homemaker crockery – backstamp crude, weight too heavy.
- 'Art Deco' china figures, often with no make – colours too bright, moulding clumsy.
- 'Art Deco' ivory and bronze figures – actually made of resin or, better quality, spelter versions.

BUYING FURNITURE

- I love buying furniture at car boots, but I see so many people buying from appearance alone. You need to do more than just look at it. The following might help:
- Is it fit for the intended purpose? Will a chair bear your weight or can you even fit into it? This is especially true of spindly Edwardian versions, as we're a bit better proportioned nowadays.
- Turn chairs over before buying them to check that they have support and not just padding.
- Are the legs even and strong enough, are they broken, or have they been repaired? This can be corrected, but will cost money. Ask yourself if is there enough profit in it, even if you already know decent restorers.
- Wickerwork. Is it perfect or frayed and will it support anyone's weight? Expect to pay £60-plus per seat to repair. That's not the back, just the seat of the chair. A costly mistake to make unless it's a particularly good chair.
- Rockers. Do they rock and roll or are they stuck? Consider whether they are too low for comfort, especially if buying for yourself.
- Do the drawers of chests and bureaux pull out easily or are they stuck? Or, worse, do they fall apart when removed completely?

BUYING CLOCKS AND WATCHES

There are specialist repairers, but remember these cost money so can harm potential profit.
- Do the clocks have keys? If so, do they fit?
- Do the clocks and watches work? Ask to have them wound up to find out. Never wind without permission to avoid being accused of

over-winding. Allow the timepiece to run for at least five minutes before buying. Do the hands move? Do they carry on ticking? Some might tick for a couple of minutes – long enough for some people to buy – but that's as far as they go.

- Do the parts move when they should?
- Is there a pendulum?
- Should it have other parts? Is it only the main part of a garniture, with the side parts missing, which will detract from its value, or can you sell it on its own?

BUYING GOLD, SILVER AND JEWELLERY

A large percentage of 'gold' and 'silver' sold at car boots is actually plate (or even less than that). Don't take the seller's word for it; check the hallmark before buying. EPNS means silver plate – and that's a lot cheaper than silver. Not all sellers are doing this deliberately; many just don't understand. So save money and read the signs for yourself.

However, I suggest that you do not use a hallmark book at the stall to check dates. A specialist dealer will already have the right

information. And you don't want to draw attention to a particularly good buy if purchasing from a dealer.

Never open a cabinet without permission, it can look as though you're stealing and can alienate the seller – at the expense of your potential discount.

BUYING CLOTHES AND VINTAGE ACCESSORIES

Whether for yourself or resale, there are some salient points to check:
- Stains – look under the arms for stains (and also smells) which can't be removed
- Check for holes and general wear and tear
- Look in pockets. It's interesting what gets left behind, both profitable or unwholesome on occasion (including things that can stain or smell).
- Look for discolouration – especially in sweat areas, such as the chest, armpits and thighs.
- Don't buy second-hand knickers. Do you even want to handle them?
- Decoration such as sequins etc. Look for fraying. Are there missing pieces, or could there be by the time you get home? If you're not good at repairs and are buying for yourself, don't waste your money
- Are all of the buttons there?

- Does the zip work?
- Look at cleaning instructions. Can you afford dry clean-only clothes, especially when, for hygiene reasons, they'll need cleaning as soon as you buy them? Expect to pay around £60 to dry clean a leather coat. That bargain might not be such a good buy after all.
- If dry cleaning, remove stylish or decorated buttons before taking them in or they could be ruined – as would your potential designer clothes profit margin.
- There are some fab vintage clothes at car boots and they're so cheap. I paid 20p for a genuine 1960s dress from Biggleswade car boot because someone was clearing out her house and she'd had it since it was new.
- Vintage accessories are also good buys but, if buying compacts, be careful when opening so you're not covered in powder. Also check that the mirror is still there and isn't damaged or worn.

CHILDREN'S GOODS AND CLOTHES

Think Health and Safety as well as hygiene when buying children's goods. Anything too chewed or scrappy is best left. Also, check:
- Toys for riding – how stable are they? Will they bear your child's weight or are wheels too loose or wobbly?

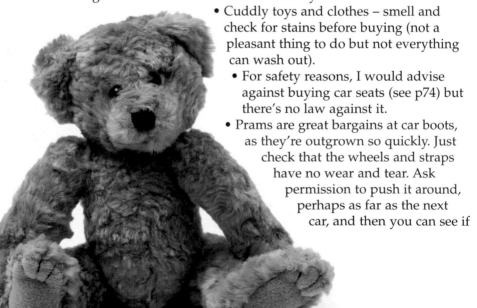

- Cuddly toys and clothes – smell and check for stains before buying (not a pleasant thing to do but not everything can wash out).
- For safety reasons, I would advise against buying car seats (see p74) but there's no law against it.
- Prams are great bargains at car boots, as they're outgrown so quickly. Just check that the wheels and straps have no wear and tear. Ask permission to push it around, perhaps as far as the next car, and then you can see if

it runs smoothly or gravitates to one side. But don't just take it
without permission or the seller could wonder what you're doing.

- Toys are good to buy at car boots as they're so expensive to buy
  new. But just ask if all the pieces are there if buying board games,
  jigsaws, etc.
- If buying cycles, check the tyres, seat, brakes and handles – do they
  gravitate to one side, are they safe? If in doubt, don't risk it.

ELECTRICAL GOODS AND MOBILE PHONES

I've bought some very good bargains, including Scart leads and boxes,
all for at least five times less than I'd have to pay at shops. If buying
electrical goods, ask the following:

- Can you see them working? If not, don't buy – someone's word
  isn't good enough when you'll never see them again.
- If being sold by a dealer, ask about warranties,
  but don't expect to get them at car boots.
- Don't let the seller out of your sight once
  you have chosen the item, because goods
  can get swapped. Check before paying
  that what should be in the box is
  actually in it – and just walk away if
  not. Dodgy dealers don't expect to be
  caught out until the buyers get
  home, By then, it's too late.
- Never arrange to meet someone
  you've first met at a car boot and
  buy electrical goods from them
  away from a business venue
  such as a warehouse or
  another car boot.
- Mobile phones are readily
  available, especially from
  specialist dealers. Ask
  for proof that they

Check that games are complete before buying them.

work before buying and don't buy if they say the battery isn't charged or it's on a different network. You could be lumbered with a barred, stolen phone.

AND FINALLY

Just be sensible. If you don't trust the seller, even if you seem to be looking at a great bargain, ask yourself what worries you. If your concerns feel legitimate (especially if buying electrical goods or mobiles), walk away. It's your money; don't throw it away. But, ultimately, car boots are fantastic places for good bargains. Yes, there's a load of tat as well, but there's always something good to find, even if it's not what you set out to buy. Just enjoy it!

CHAPTER 8

GOING HOME

BEFORE you leave, don't forget to do the following:
- Collect all of your goods.
- Speak to the dealers you liked and ask where else they pitch, so you can find out which other car boots are worth visiting.
- Ensure that all of your buys are properly packed in the wrapping which you brought with you and, if necessary, put in boxes or wedged in so they don't roll and break or distract you when you're driving.
- Leave before the car boot ends to avoid the inevitable queues.
- Be patient as there will be some drivers out there who jump queues and go down different rows to beat the system. It doesn't matter; you'll still get out.
- There are some fairs where it's very hard to turn against the traffic as you exit. Just go left and then turn around at a roundabout or road junction. You can get stuck for ages otherwise (this being especially true of Denham car boot).
- And keep a beady eye out for signs for another car boot on the way home.

Find out where your favourite car booters will be the following week and which other car boots they recommend. I loved this stall with its Merrythought toys and Bunnykins and found out which regular car boots the dealers use so that I can buy from them again.

SELLING AT CAR BOOTS

Maximise your profits by grouping items together and making your pitch look appealing to buyers, as seen with this stall at Ford, Sussex.

CHAPTER 1

WHY DO A
CAR BOOT SALE?

T HERE are many reasons to take a pitch at a car boot, which is why thousands of people do it every year, especially on hot summer weekends. Some are professional sellers (car booters, market traders, antiques traders, specialist dealers) whilst others just do one or two in their lifetime to clear excess goods. But why do they do it?

- To clear excess belongings such as crockery, mobile phones, clothes, toys etc. and get paid for it.
- For quick and easy money with cash sales.
- It is half a day's work.
- It can mean easy money for your summer holiday or unexpected household bills.
- Kids grow fast so you can make money by selling their old clothes, shoes and toys and spend the income on clothes which fit.
- Car boots are the perfect place to raise money for redecorating your house by selling the unwanted curtains, rugs, crockery etc. which won't work with the new design or colour scheme.
- The pitches are cheap compared to markets and antiques fairs.
- You can save on petrol if attending a local venue, though you will have to travel to attend some of the bigger ones.
- Car boots are organised, advertised events with stewards, a set time and place, toilets and food and drink vans so buyers know to attend.
- It is enjoyable to work in the sun if you are lucky enough to have good weather.
- The events can provide a sociable activity.
- They are an easy but profitable part-time or summer business. Few car boots operate year-round but it's a great way to earn extra money.

- There is the opportunity to sell off unwanted Christmas or birthday presents and spend the money on something you really want.
- Boot fairs are an enjoyable, stress-free way of trying out the antiques business without high stall rents or long days. A new phenomenum is the large number of new antique dealers who started out as professional car booters, learning how to buy and sell with minimal time and expense.
- Unlike markets where buyers have a shopping list in mind, people tend to potter around car boots so impulse buying is higher.
- There are different types of sellers from those attending many local markets, which attracts more buyers.
- Many markets are mid-week and car boots open up the weekend trade.
- People go willing to spend money on bargains, producing the right mind-set to sell cheaper-end goods.
- Car boots are a good place to sell the remainder of auction job lots. More choice items can go to antiques fairs and other auctions.

If everything really must go, let people know. That way, you won't be taking unwanted goods home at the end of the day.

- It is a great chance to get rid of tired stock. Even if you struggled to sell your lower-end goods at an antiques fair, you might make more at a car boot. It is a different market, and fresh stock as far as buyers there are concerned.

Antiques fairs are slow in summer and stall rent is considerably higher than at car boots. But they are a good option on wet weekends and with the right goods. Buy cheaply at car boots, and sell the items alongside your own goods at antiques fairs during colder months for higher profits.

CAR BOOT TIPS

Expect to pay £6-£12 for a pitch. Vans will be charged around a third more than cars at most venues. Not all events allow vans, however, so check before setting out. A trailer will cost about £2 extra.

What are your other options?

Car boots are not the only places to sell or get rid of excess belongings or collectables. You can also sell at:

Antiques fairs[1] v Car Boot

Pros

- More knowledgeable buyers who pay more.
- Better place to sell quality goods.
- Mainly indoor events so protection against the weather.
- If outdoor fairs, space and time to pitch marquees.
- Set stalls so buyers know where to find you every time.

Cons

- Higher stall rent.
- Longer days.
- Payment isn't always cash.
- Generally have to travel, incurring higher petrol costs.

Auctions[2] v Car Boot

Pros

- Your goods should realise at least market value.
- Valuations by experts so you don't accidentally sell a rare antique, toy or record at a car boot.
- Open to competition with buyers raising bids against each other, not just the set car boot price which goes down with haggling.
- No dealing with buyers direct.
- No early morning starts.
- Rain won't stop play.

Cons

- Expect to wait 21 days for payment and for the cheque to clear.
- Commission (generally 10-15% but can be higher at some auction houses. There may also be set minimum commissions), VAT on commission and any lottage or insurance cuts into your profit margin.

---

1 See *How to Deal in Antiques* by Fiona Shoop (How To Books, 4th edition, 2009).
2 See *How to Profit from... Auctions* by Fiona Shoop (Remember When, 2009).

Antiques Centres v Car Boot

PROS

- Often very well advertised.
- Regular buyers.
- Depending on the centre, you don't need to be there or sell to the buyers yourself (manned centres only).
- No early morning starts.
- Goods are out on display so there's no need to pack and unpack everything in one day.
- Unpack and change stock in your own time.

CONS

- Needs a commitment (proper labelling, regular change of stock, etc.).
- Stall rent and commission cut into profits.
- Often a drive away from home so petrol costs can be high.

eBay v Car Boot

PROS

- Competition could drive up prices.
- No early morning start.
- Make money in your pyjamas.
- Money takes a few days to come in after theuploading time.
- Worldwide market.

CONS

- Takes time to upload information and take photographs.
- You can easily sell more at a car boot whereas eBay involves multi-day auctions.
- Postage and packaging costs have to be calculated.
- You have to post the goods and not all on one day as auctions will be staggered and payments are made at different times.
- Fees can really add up compared to a one-off car boot sale pitch.
- Not as sociable as car boots.

Internet Car Boots (see p160) v Car Boot

PROS

- Advertised in car boot press.
- 24-hour car boot.
- Weather-proof.
- No early morning starts.

CONS

- Not as good as eBay.
- Prices are often unrealistic.
- Lack of wide marketing reflected in poor number of buyers.

Jumble Sales v Car Boot

PROS

- Indoor events.
- Cheap entrance fee attracts buyers.

CONS

- Not as common as they were.
- All profits might have to be given to charity.

Garage Sales v Car Boot

PROS

- No petrol costs.
- Set up in your own time if you can close off the drive until the start time.
- No pitch rent or competition.
- In one go, can sell more items than would fit in a car or ones too large to transport.

CONS

- You have to advertise it (time and money).
- People come to your home.
- Limited parking could deter buyers and annoy neighbours.
- Can get too busy to control so you lose buyers or goods might get stolen

(there are more stalls at car boots so everyone isn't buying from you at the same time).

- In contrast, too few people could turn up as there's only one 'stall'.
- You need to have help from friends or family.
- Can be awkward having neighbours going through your belongings.

Notice in newsagents window, local supermarket or in the classified ad section v Car Boot

PROS

- Sell larger items.
- Sell single items.
- No early morning starts.
- Minimal cost.

CONS

- Do you want people coming to your home?
- Some 'buyers' can use this information to find out when you're out or to look at what you DON'T want to part with. Be very careful what you say and never let people know when you're always out ('I never get home before 6pm' etc)
- Personally, I wouldn't sell this way but that's my choice, I just don't want strangers in my home. Nor do my Dobermans…
- Be careful if you have children. It can be an invitation to the wrong sort of person, especially if you're out a lot or a single mother. That's why you shouldn't sell children's goods this way.

Markets v Car Boot

PROS

- Established venues so people know where and when they are.
- Well organised events.
- Sociable, regular buyers and sellers.
- Year-round so regular income.
- Established facilities.

Cons

- Have to repark car after unloading at the start of the day and fetch it at the end, leaving goods unattended.
- Parking fees can be an issue.
- Stall rent can be high.
- You might not be allowed to sell there if types or numbers of similar stalls are limited.
- Year-round, so there is an obligation to stall, even on cold or wet days, to keep your pitch.

House Clearance v Car Boot

Pros

- You can get paid for all of your goods to be taken away

Cons

- You won't get as much as it's worth, but they collect everything in one go (or two) so it's out of the way.
- Some now charge to take away your goods and then sell them on for a profit.

Charity Shops v Car Boot

Pros

- Support good causes
- Everything can go at once (if they accept it – see below).

Cons

- No money for you.
- Often not even a thank you or help carrying goods in.
- Few charities can now afford to collect goods themselves so you have to take them there and unload them.
- They can reject items which is humiliating and insulting.

The Dump / Bin / Recycling Centres v Car Boot

PROS ☑

- It's all gone.
- Recycling is good for the environment.

CONS ☒

- No money.
- What a waste of potential profit and the chance for other people to re-use your goods.
- Time-consuming as you have to put everything in different areas of the dump and they search your goods.
- Can fill your bin at home too quickly.
- Not good if collections are fortnightly.
- Queues for the dump are long at weekends.

Why do a car boot sale?

Ultimately, to make money without having to work too hard, and to clear belongings or stock. It's also worth remembering that although you're there to sell, you can also buy as well. That gives you the opportunity to both make money and extra profits.

Car boot tips

I always check the stalls around me when I'm selling. You're likely to get chatting to your neighbours anyway, but see what they're selling. I bet your discounts are higher than anyone just wandering up to buy. I bought virtually all the china off a stall opposite me at one car boot, and they were really surprised. But I knew what they had and how much I could make, which was more than ten times what they were charging. I just had to make sure I sold enough that day so I had enough room in my car to take all the china home.

AND FINALLY...

One, small point. You need to own a car or van, or at least access to one, to stall at a car boot. It seems obvious, but it is surprising that not everyone thinks it through. Do you want to sell larger items? Will they fit in your car? Load the car the night before, to ensure everything fits in. But if you don't feel safe in your area, unload it and reload in the morning. Not all areas are suitable for leaving cars filled with interesting items overnight.

CHAPTER 2

REGISTRATION ACTS

WHERE YOU NEED TO REGISTER BEFORE BECOMING A REGULAR CAR BOOTER

D ID YOU know that you are required to register with some Trading Standards offices before becoming a regular car booter? It's amazing how many people don't, and organisers often don't think to mention it because the Registration Acts have been around for years. But they affect second-hand dealers, including regular car booters.

DO I NEED TO REGISTER?

If you are only doing one or two car boots to sell your goods, you generally don't need to register. But if you're selling in any of the areas mentioned (see p113), check with the organisers first, simply because Trading Standards officers are very active. You might just be intending to stall out once or twice, but they could be the very times when the Trading Standards people see you. As a basic rule, clearing out your own home with one or two car boots is fine. Any more and you should register. It's normally free, but you will need to be aware of the terms of trading as frustratingly, they differ from area to area.

WHAT TYPE OF PEOPLE NEED TO REGISTER?

Many types of second-hand dealers, including car booters and antique dealers. Some of the selling laws exempt certain types of traders, such as scrap-metal and second-hand book dealers. Interestingly, in Scotland, car booters and antique dealers come under the same category as tanners and sex shop owners! The basic principle is that people who earn their living, or have a part-time business selling second-hand goods, need to register with Trading Standards in every area where there is a relevant Act. Every area has different rules requiring different types of paperwork. Once you get used to it, it's fine but you do need to know who needs what and where.

How will this affect me?

If you are intending to be a regular car booter or sell at antiques fairs or markets in the areas listed (see p113), register with Trading Standards beforehand. In most places, there is no fee but you do need to be aware of what is required, as it differs significantly from area to area. The most important elements concern identification and paperwork. Always carry the Registration Certificate with you (when there is one) and, if required, display it in your car window when selling at car boots.

If you're not intending to sell, but just buy, still be aware that those selling to you might need to ask for your contact details to fulfil the terms of the Registration Acts. If you're not happy with someone needing your details and have verified why they need them, either don't buy the goods or give your work address. I always gave the address of an antiques centre where I had a stall. Like you, I don't want a stranger knowing where I live, but some of the Acts do require full paperwork. Others don't need to know the details of the buyer.

Will there ever be a nationwide registration act for car boots?

I hope not. When I was writing about The Kent County Council Act for various publications, including The *Antiques Trade Gazette* back in 2001, it was seen as a test case, ready for rolling out nationwide. There hasn't been any obvious movement since, but you never know. That said, for those of you who need to register, it would help if every area needed exactly the same paperwork to make it easier for professional car booters and antique dealers who sell all over the country.

The Registration Acts

In alphabetical order, (apart from, Scotland), the counties or areas where you must register before car booting or dealing antiques on a regular basis, (i.e. not just to clear your home) are:

- Greater Manchester
- Hereford City
- Humberside
- Kent
- Lancashire
- Merseyside
- Newcastle
- Worcester City
- Yorkshire (South)
- Yorkshire (North)

The whole of Scotland is covered by a Registration Act, whilst some cities, such as Glasgow, also have their own registration requirements. Ask before trading

WHERE TO REGISTER

Speak to the car boot organisers or Trading Standards in the county or area. Those wishing to trade in Glasgow, should also speak to the market organisers if intending to have a pitch there, as they have a separate registration rule.

If in doubt, just ask the organisers at car boots or markets when you book, as it's in their interests for all of their pitch-holders to be registered. For car boots, ring the organisers in advance so you can go elsewhere if necessary.

CAN I JUST NOT REGISTER?

It's not worth it. You could get caught and fined, and possibly even banned from selling in the area if you are a repeat offender. There are two ways to deal with the need to register. Either do it or just don't trade in the areas if you feel opposed to the regulation. But, as Trading Standards officers and the police are regular visitors to car boots, and as the organisers need to keep their business, just don't risk getting caught – especially in areas where it's free to register. After the initial outcry, I don't know any dealer who has had a problem in Kent, where the rules turned out to be far easier and less intrusive than expected, after changes were made to the original regulations.

Indoor or under-cover car boots are worth considering during the early car boot season. This photo was taken at a car boot in late–April when the weather was still too unpredictable for regular and profitable outdoor selling.

CHAPTER 3

FINDING THE RIGHT CAR BOOT SALE

THIS isn't as obvious as it might sound. It's not just about working out where your nearest car boot is (see p167 for the county by county directory), but what sort of goods you are selling and how you like to work.

• There are various points you need to consider:

• Indoor or outdoor – or both?

• What do you want to sell? Do the other stalls support this?

• Are there any goods you're not allowed to sell?

• How easy is it to get to?

• What's the advertising/marketing like?

• Does it have a good reputation?

• What are the buyers like?

INDOOR OR OUTDOOR – OR BOTH?

Unlike markets, car boots don't have established stalls covered with tarpaulin to protect them from the weather. Indoor car boots are the answer if it's pouring with rain. These tend to be at disused airfields with huge hangers. They are not to everyone's taste for two very good reasons: they can feel claustrophobic, and it is very hard to leave early if you're not at the end of the row.

I used to stall at Oakington, in Cambridgeshire, when I lived in a neighbouring county. The old airfield combined indoor and outdoor stalls. I stalled outdoor once and it was good, mainly because there was a hard-standing area so I didn't need to worry about being bogged down if it had rained. However, I preferred to stall in the open-ended hangar which wasn't at all claustrophobic. Unfortunately, I never left quite as early as I liked, and unless I was lucky enough to be at the end, I had to wait for several pitches to leave before reversing out. Obviously, I couldn't do this if there were buyers still around. But I always did very well at Oakington and, if it started to rain, the buyers flocked in and I carried on selling, while the outdoor stalls had to cover up. Most of them just went home. It was worth going even on wet days, and that's a huge consideration when stalling.

The negatives of indoor stalls, in my opinion, are outweighed by the positives:

Pros

- Protected from the weather, so you can still make money when it's raining.
- All buyers go inside, even if they don't make it to the furthest stalls, at rambling car boots.

Cons

- Less space. You are generally crammed in, so just have room for a paste table, folding table and your car boot. The car parked parallel is generally quite tight to you, so open your door as soon as you arrive if no one is parked there yet. It will give you enough room to manoeuvre as the other driver won't park too close.
- Can be claustrophobic.
- Can be chilly when it's sunny, as it doesn't heat up as quickly as you'd expect. Just take layers to wear but avoid drinking coffee or you'll have to leave your stall to use the facilities which vary dramatically.
- The stalls can be more market trader-style than general car boots.
- Pitch rent can be a bit higher, but, if it rains, your rent isn't wasted by having to pack up or cover goods.

GRASS VERSUS HARD-STANDING

What about outdoor car boots? The reality is that there are more outdoor than indoor ones. The ones on grass look better and feel more 'car boot' and less 'market' (so you expect to pay less as a buyer and can focus your mind on 'seeing' more bargains). But I prefer hard-standing, especially when it's been raining, as they're far less likely to be cancelled and you won't run the risk of getting bogged down and having muddy footprints on your clothes and curtains – or have books and ephemera (e.g. magazines and posters) ruined by muddy marks. It depends what is near you; what's good and what the weather has been like in the past few days. Some have a mix of grass and hard standing or indoor and out, so get to know your car boots and see what works for you.

If possible, I try to stall at car boots with a mix of indoor and outdoor stalls, or at least some hard-standing.

WHAT DO YOU WANT TO SELL?

The reason I ask this is that there are car boots where your goods just won't fit in, so you'll be wasting your time. These are the questions you need to ask if you haven't looked at the car boot scene already:

- Are there enough general car booters, or will your personal belongings not sell if it's the wrong market for them?
- Are market traders or specialist dealers allowed to sell at that car boot?
- If you're a specialist trader, (not an antique dealer), ask if you're allowed to sell there before travelling. Some car boots limit the number or type of trader allowed to sell. If they have one fruit and vegetable stall already, they might not want another, and there are venues where certain traders are banned because the field is owned by people with a competing business. For instance, you can't sell plants and cut flowers at Biggleswade car boot, because it is run by the people who own the adjacent business where they sell plants and flowers.
- Those running food and drink vans, in particular, need to check that they're welcome, as most car boots already have agreements with similar traders.

Food vendors should check that they're welcome before turning up at a car boot. Get on organisers' waiting lists to take advantage of unexpected vacancies. And don't forget to take enough oil. That is the most common mistake made by new food vendors, alongside not having enough plastic cups for selling hot drinks on cold mornings.

How easy is it to find?

I've set out for car boots and just not been able to find them, even with a map. This is especially true when signposting is poor, and the only address given is a farm on a very long road. If the event isn't popular, there won't be any long queues to follow. Always try to visit a car boot before stalling there for the first time to assess its suitability, including whether you can even find it. If you can't, what about other buyers?

ADVERTISING AND MARKETING

These aren't the same. Advertising is paid for space, and even home-made road signs count as advertising. Do they take out ads in the local paper? Are they in the car boot press and websites? Not just *Car Boot and Fairs Calendar* but other places such as www.carbootjunction.com or the *Friday Ads*? If they don't try to attract buyers in the trade press, how will people know they are there?

Marketing is more than just advertising, vital though that is. Do they get mentioned in articles? Do they work to attract publicity? I'm surprised how few do. I haven't had a press release about a car boot sale since I edited the now defunct *Antiques & Collectables*, when there was a car boot at a stately home. Even when I do radio shows about car boots, the producers have to ask me to recommend a couple so they can get organisers or regular car booters on the show and that's because too many car boot organisers rely on word of mouth or homemade road signs to attract buyers and sellers.

The bottom line is that if people don't know about an irregular or new venue, how are the organisers expecting to attract buyers? Road signs are all very well, but what if it's the road less travelled? These are questions you need to ask organisers – if you can find their details, that is.

Thankfully, more and more have realised the advantages of websites to advertise their events, especially if they run more than one. They also use them to advertise irregular or special events, and to state whether the boot sale has been cancelled due to the weather or other problems.

CAR BOOT TIPS

Traditional car booters (i.e. those selling excess belongings) should look at car boots before deciding to stall there, to see if there are more market traders than people selling their own clothes, books etc. You could be wasting your time and money otherwise.

Reputation

That said, word of mouth is often the best way to discover new car boots. Everyone told me to go to Denham (for details, see p170) when I was reviewing fairs and car boots for a variety of publications, including The *Antiques Trade Gazette* and the now defunct *The Dealer*. I went to write about it, loved it and became a regular. That's what a reputation can do for a car boot. We also hear about which ones to avoid (poor organisation, no advertising, no road signs, poor facilities and bad buyers).

What are the buyers like?

This is a great generalisation, but it can depend on the area. It's not just to do with money (can they afford what you want to sell?) but other factors. Do you want your neighbours rummaging through your goods? Are they expecting to pay decent money at a car boot, or is it a '£1 and under' venue? Are they only after new, market goods? Go as a buyer and see if you want to be a seller.

And that's the real point. As with any venue for any business, check it out before investing your time and money. Do you like it? Was it easy to drive there or did you get lost? Was there proper signage? Did your car or others get stuck in the mud? Was the track too uneven for you to want to drive over it with breakables? Or did you love it and buy so much that you don't want to go as a seller in case you miss more great bargains as a buyer?

CHAPTER 4

PREPARATION

Y OU CAN'T really wake up one morning and decide to do a car boot unless you've done them before, and unless you have your goods ready. Instead, spend the day before getting ready so you are all prepared and won't make costly mistakes. Or have a 'car boot bag' on hand so, if you do wake up early and the weather is good, you can just get going. That's what I always do. And don't forget to clean your goods before the sale. They'll look more appealing and hygienic that way.

THE BASICS

There are certain goods that you'll need at every car boot. Some of this has been covered before, but use this as a checklist for your next (or first) car boot:

- A bag of change. Take a lot of change with you, especially 50ps, £1 and £5 notes, but also a few £10 notes as well. It's surprising how fast this goes. Top up your float every Monday when you bank your takings, so it's always ready for those impulse car boots.
- Carrier bags. Just reuse supermarket ones. Unless you are a market trader, you probably don't need to buy any, but if you do, get them cheaply from shop suppliers or even at car boots. I pay £1 for a pack of around 50-100.
- Wrapping. Save your money. Don't buy tissue paper, but use newspaper instead. Always take a bundle of unused papers with you, as there is never enough at the end of the day, or, hopefully, during it. It just stops goods from breaking en route and keeps your buyers happy.
- Water. I simply reuse water bottles, or those that contained other drinks, and refill them from the tap. On very hot days, I put one in the freezer the night before, so it's lovely and chilled even in the sun when it's partly melted. This saves a fortune on drinks at the venue

and means I don't have to miss sales by queuing for what are often over-priced drinks.

- Sandwiches and snacks. You can get tired quickly with the early starts and unpacking, so take energy bars, snacks or sandwiches with you. Again, this saves time and money as you won't have to leave your stall.
- Wet wipes and other types of wet tissues. Your hands get dirty fairly quickly if you are handling newspaper, and wipes refresh throughout the day so you don't have to leave your stall. They are also useful if you buy dirty china and glass etc at the car boot and want to sell it on immediately for a profit. A quick wipe and it looks worth far more than you've paid.
- Tissues. Another useful cleaning method, and unlike cloths, they don't need washing. They are also great for runny noses and wiping mud off shoes when the grass is wet.
- A chair. So many people forget to take chairs when doing car boots. You'll need one for each person stalling. I'd also recommend taking a spare for good buyers to sit on whilst you're wrapping their goods or they're counting out their money. Expect neighbours to want to borrow one, so if your car is big enough, take another one for them as well. It means you still have a chair for customers, but keeps your neighbour happy too, meaning they will be inclined to watch your stall when you go to the loo – via other stalls. Don't expect to sit on your car seat or in the boot. You might not have enough room, and the door blocks out what's happening down the end of the stall. It's also not that comfortable.
- Tables. You need sturdy tables at car boots. Some people forget to bring any, and end up selling off the ground or from a cloth on the ground. It's not ideal when selling china and other breakables, which can fall and chip if they're not standing on a level surface. I use a sturdy paste table, readily available from DIY outlets. Mine has a bar across each side for extra strength. Be wary of any which sag in the middle without this extra support, as your potential profits could literally be smashing. I actually use two paste tables, one in front of the other, and a folding table for the end of the stall. If there's space, I have a cloth on the floor for books.
- If you're selling clothes on a regular basis, invest in a clothes rack which can be bought from DIY outlets and stores like Argos. This

Maximise your profits by being organised. This fishing tackle stand had everything in the right place for fast unpacking, and bags and leaflets at the ready for fast sales and future profits.

makes the clothes look more appealing and they will more easily when displayed professionally.

- Hangers. Many car booters hang clothes and curtains over their car door or boots. But hangers keep them clean, and are easier to use than trying to drape them over doors. They invariably slip and fall on the ground otherwise, leaving you with muddy or dusty goods, forcing you to knock down the price.
- Layers. Take extra tops to wear as it's colder in the morning than you'd think. You can then peel layers off when it gets hot in the afternoon.
- Hats. To keep warm in cold weather and to prevent sunstroke when it is hot.
- Wellies. In case the field is muddy. You'll need them if you have to go to the toilet or out buying.
- A notebook. This enables you to keep track of your sales and to write receipts if buyers want them. You could spend money on a receipt book if you're a professional car booter, trader or dealer. You will need records of sales for the tax office if you're doing car boots on a regular basis or are stalling in a Registration Act area (see p113).
- Pens. To keep a record of your sales.
- A calculator. For adding up sales for buyers and for your end of day total for yourself.
- Newspaper or book. To keep you entertained at quiet times. But only use when no one is around or you could lose sales.
- Cloth. To make use of extra space on the floor whilst keeping your goods clean.
- Labels. Tie-on and sticky just in case you buy extra goods, or need to change labels on the day. This could be because it is wet and the ink has run, the writing is not as legible as it could be, or simply because a label has come off.

Business cards

Not many regular car booters bother with business cards unless they have another business (e.g. shop or are also antique dealers). That's because people can find them at the same event every week, and they don't want to be disturbed in between. Most regulars build up a steady clientele who know exactly where to find them. It's entirely up

Did you know?

The money you make at car boots is known as 'takings', just like in a shop. But remember, if you do this regularly, sadly it's not tax-free (see p163).

to you if you want to use cards or not. If you do, only give a mobile number, and if you want, an e-mail address.

Never use your home address on a card as people know that you're not around when the car boot's on. I also never give a home number, so people don't ring at unsociable times – especially if you get up really early to do car boots. You might even choose to have one mobile specifically for the car boot season. It is tax deductible if you do (see p163).

It's up to you. There is no right and wrong here, unlike with antiques fairs where you should have one. Pitches selling new specialist goods, such as the fishing tackle stand pictured, should have leaflets with prices or business cards printed for return and for future customers who can buy from them at a later date.

MONEY SAFETY

I'm always shocked at the number of women I see at car boots who use handbags for their takings, and then tuck them in their open car boot before leaving them to serve someone at the far end of their pitch. I wear a bum bag ('fanny bag' for American readers) or even a market trader belt with two large pockets in front. Handbags do get stolen at car boots because they're so incredibly accessible. I also keep my money in several purses, so I don't flash a wodge at anyone. It also means I don't look like I'm doing too well when refusing to give huge discounts.

PREPARING GOODS

Start off by deciding what to sell. Obviously, this is different for market traders who know their buyers and take exactly the same type of stock to car boots as they do to their regular markets. For everyone else, including antique dealers, read on:

Selling your personal belongings

If you're selling your own goods, make a pile of it at home, put it into bags and boxes and then start sorting through it. Here are some basic tips to the general items people sell at car boots when clearing their own goods.

Clothes

DON'T give away profits, check your pockets

If selling clothes, make sure they're clean, but don't waste money dry cleaning 'dry clean only' clothes. Always check pockets, as it's surprising how many unexpected good buys I've had at car boots. Buyers can't take the money or jewellery back to the sellers as they might not be there again. And do you remember everyone from whom you've bought? I certainly don't. Don't give away profits, just check your pockets.

If possible, have set prices for clothes and write them on a piece of cardboard instead of labelling everything individually which takes time. This way, the would-be buyer can see immediately if they want to pay what you're charging e.g. 50p for tops, £2 for skirts, £10 for leather jackets, or whatever. If selling designer clothes, make it obvious that they're good makes, by pricing them separately. Also make this clear on the label for other goods (e.g. designer clothes priced individually). This also draws attention to the idea that you've got some Jaeger or Calvin Klein lurking amongst everything else which will get the buyers drooling.

But price realistically, as clothes can be slow to sell, especially as buyers generally can't try them on. Would you trust them to return after taking a handful to the dirty toilets to 'try on'? I'm a cynic. I wouldn't expect to see them again, but judge each buyer for yourself, or price to sell.

If selling clothes regularly at car boots, invest in a clothes rail where your clothes will look better and be more accessible for people who don't have time or the inclination to rummage for great buys. And, whatever you do, don't tell people it won't fit them because they're 'too fat'. Just don't commit yourself, but say something pleasant like, 'The colour really suits you'.

BOOKS

If selling books, save time and write a sign on the box they are in or on a bit of cardboard with two prices for hardbacks and paperbacks. It's up to you what you charge, but you want to sell them, so stick to £2 or under for normal hardbacks, and 20p-50p for paperbacks. I buy a lot

Price books realistically so they sell. I paid 50p each for these Alison Uttley books at a car boot and can resell them at £2-£3 each on the internet. As they were good value, I bought 11 of them but wouldn't have bought so many if they'd been more expensive as I have to take the cost of my time and petrol into account when reselling – as will your buyers.

of books at car boots, but find that people clearing their houses or even professional, non-specialist car booters, charge far too much for often scrappy second-hand books. Just get rid of them.

Alternatively, sell them for more money on Amazon (www.amazon.co.uk), Abe Books (www.abebooks.co.uk) or eBay, (www.ebay.co.uk), where you generally get more money for books than car boots. But remember if you do this, you have to sort out envelopes, postage costs and then post them. If selling children's books more than around 20 years old, hardback versions of Philip Pullman, J. K. Rowling, or the early books of now best-selling crime writers, check that they're not first editions or you could be selling thousands of pounds worth of books for less than £2.

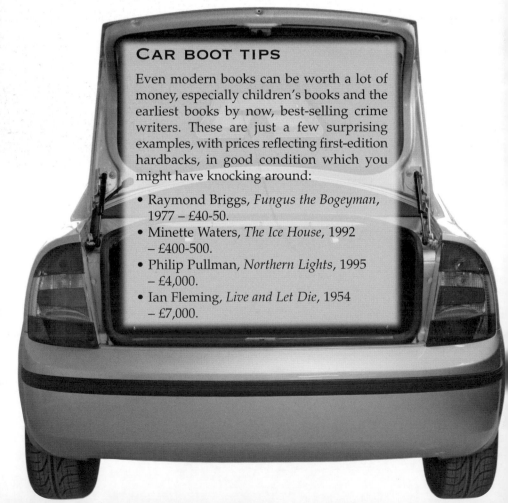

CAR BOOT TIPS

Even modern books can be worth a lot of money, especially children's books and the earliest books by now, best-selling crime writers. These are just a few surprising examples, with prices reflecting first-edition hardbacks, in good condition which you might have knocking around:

- Raymond Briggs, *Fungus the Bogeyman*, 1977 – £40-50.
- Minette Waters, *The Ice House*, 1992 – £400-500.
- Philip Pullman, *Northern Lights*, 1995 – £4,000.
- Ian Fleming, *Live and Let Die*, 1954 – £7,000.

By boxing these children's clothes into age groups, the seller will attract busy parents who don't have time to sift through huge piles of kids' clothing at car boots. This is a great way to maximise your profits or, if a buyer, find quality apparel to sell on eBay for even more money.

CHILDREN'S GOODS

Put children's toys and clothes in boxes, and write the prices on the side. For example: toy cars, 50p; children's clothes, aged 8-12 months, £1 each; or whatever. But please check the toys you're selling. If recent, that's fine, but if they were yours or your partner's when they were young, check that you're not selling rare Dinkys or dolls etc. Have a quick peek at eBay (www.ebay.co.uk) or Vectis (www.vectis.co.uk) or visit your local auction house[1] for advice.

1 See *How to Profit from … Auctions* by Fiona Shoop (Remember When, 2009) for a county-by-county directory of auction houses.

Records and CDs

Records sell well at car boots. but I'd check them all first. Did you hear the one about the seller who sold an autographed Rolling Stones album for £2 when it was really worth £4,000? Don't let that be your mistake. Check first. There are price guides for record collections. These are the few price guides that I actually rate, but use them to check relative, not exact values, as they do change. It just gives an idea of rarity.

CDs can become unfashionable and 'date' very quickly, so price them according to popularity – 20p for ones you don't want to admit ever owning, and around 50p-£1 for normal ones. I've paid £3 before if I've really wanted one, but from professional car booters who have a great selection. Just sell them off at a realistic sum and make money to buy new ones or you could get stuck with them.

Check that you're not giving someone else a fortune. Read up on record prices before selling your old LPs at car boots. Invest in a price guide.

HOUSEHOLD CROCKERY AND KITCHEN PARAPHERNALIA

Sell cheaply for maximum sales. Your old mugs are not highly desirable unless by makes like Portmeirion. The same goes for saucepans and kettles, or even that unopened fondue set you were given years ago. Price to sell and clear out your cupboards.

COLLECTABLES

This is a difficult area as you might not realise what you have or (the other danger) if you do, will try to get your money back or make a good profit. Just be realistic. If it's worth £50, price it at £20-£30 and it will sell. Stick £50 on and you'll be stuck with it. Anything good (or you suspect to be good), put into auction, or do an antiques fair. Otherwise, price to sell – but don't forget to check for damage before

Collectables sell very well at car boots but make sure you know what you're selling and its true value. This is a car boot, so don't overprice collectables or give away potential profits. The lamp shades on the left would sell for around £80-£120 the pair on a retro stall at an antiques fair. They're wasted at car boots where, realistically, they'd fetch around £20-£30 the pair, if that.

selling, or you could be stuck with damaged goods, priced as perfect. Wade Whimsies aren't what they used to be, so expect to get 50p-£1 these days for the 1970s/80s versions.

FURNITURE

Empty all drawers (it's surprising how many people don't) and then dust and polish, if applicable. The better it looks, the more you'll get. And always price furniture to save time-wasters and speed up sales. Price to sell. Vintage, unless designer, is seen as cheap tat at car boots, so price to sell or you could be taking it home. I buy small chests of drawers for around £3 at car boots, and even wooden rocking chairs go for around £5. Avoid selling good quality pine or other wooden furniture or designer 1950s pieces at car boots. These are best sold at auction for maximum profits – unless you're a regular car booter/dealer and know there are the right buyers at the venue. They take up a lot of room in your car, which is best filled with lots of cheaper goods that often add up to more than the price of the piece of furniture.

Redecorating your house or moving home? Get money for unwanted furniture at car boots if your vehicle is big enough. It's the best venue for non-antique or collectable furniture.

TO LABEL OR NOT?

It depends on what you're selling and on your memory. If everything's priced, you look too professional, so some buyers will move on, assuming you know what you're doing and that there won't be any bargains. I'd advise general signs for clothes and books, and see how everything else goes. You could always keep a list behind the stall to remind yourself what you've said, especially if you're likely to get flustered by dealers or over-eager, aggressive buyers. Price larger pieces, such as furniture, to save time.

ANTIQUE DEALERS

Antique dealers should sell their lesser-end goods, normally £35 or under, for best sales and get rid of stale stock to release money for fresh goods. Remember, not everyone brings huge amounts of money to standard car boots. Having said which, vast ones like Denham (see p170) are different and people expect to spend more, so take higher-priced stock accordingly.

Next, change your labels. We know you're professionals, but you don't want novice buyers and collectors to know that. Why? Because they'll want to think they know more than you, and have discovered bargain buys. A label saying exactly what is it, a date and the price, plus professional symbols (e.g. T2 meaning you'll discount the price by £2) will deter some buyers, even if it's a really good price. They'll assume that, as a professional antique dealer, you know exactly what the goods are worth, and they're not getting a bargain.

Perception is an important part of car booting so make everyone's choices easier by using simple labels, if any, and just put prices on them. There should be no trade symbols or even words (e.g. Royal Doulton), just the price. Look like an amateur and you'll make more money. Even other dealers will be fooled if they don't know you, and you'll sell more that way.

CHAPTER 5

WHAT TO SELL

W ITH the exception of the goods listed in the next chapter, and any banned by the organisers (generally aimed more at market traders, see p140, and anyone intending to sell food, see p117), you can sell virtually anything at car boot sales. Your tat is someone else's treasure. That said, there is a basic list of what you can't sell at a car boot (see p141), mainly based on legal requirements and Health and Safety laws but, apart from these, anything goes.

WHAT CAN YOU SELL?

Really, apart from the above, you can sell virtually anything, including:

- Children's clothes. For maximum sales and profits, clean them first and then put them in boxes clearly marked with the age groups covered – e.g. 3-6 months in one box, 12-18 months in another. It saves parents from rummaging through a huge, messy pile and giving up before spending anything. Plus it's easier and neater for you to display, so won't take up as much room on your pitch.
- Children's toys. Save time and recoup some money by selling the toys that your kids have outgrown (and buy some new ones for them from neighbouring stands).
- Books. Price sensibly any that you don't want to read again, for maximum sales, or you could get stuck with them (see p127).
- Magazines. Instead of recycling them or giving them to your doctors' surgery, bundle them up and sell 10 old mags for 10p-50p. Especially sought after are bridal magazines which you don't need any longer; they're so expensive that you could get 30p-50p each if they're not too old. This might not sound much but it really does add up.
- Clothes. Losing or gaining weight, and changing tastes, mean you probably have a stash of clothes bundled at the back of your

drawers or in a cupboard. Empty your drawers and make money by selling them at a car boot. Remember to empty your pockets first. Out of date clothes? That's 'retro' to others, so empty out your wardrobe. Even your old undies will sell, as long as they don't have holes...

- Empty perfume bottles. These can fetch 50p each to collectors. Recycling can be profitable.
- Curtains. Sell unwanted curtains or nets when redecorating, for a fresh, clutter-free look to your home.
- Crockery and glasses. We all have glasses and plates we just don't ever get round to using. Free up cupboard space and make money. Raid your kitchen cupboards and make money from unused teapots, fondue sets (they're at every car boot for a reason) and other space-using kitchen goods.

Before selling your old toys, make sure they're not worth anything. It might not look much but this is a 1950s pyjama case. Poodles were very popular then and it's worth £20-£30. I paid 50p for it at Denham car boot.

- Tourist tat. That china donkey seemed such a good idea after a couple of Sangrias. Let it go at a car boot and start saving for your next holiday. Yes, people really do buy strangers' memories and bad taste.
- Mobile phones, radios etc. When you upgrade, remove your SIM and sell your old phone. Chargers also sell well as they cost so much to buy new.
- Unwanted presents. Foot spas and fondue sets.
- Wine racks and other goods which you no longer need.
- Car manuals. The Haynes manuals are another car boot regular, as well as unwanted car accessories. Empty your garage of clutter and you can actually park your car in it.
- Handbags. These do very well at car boots. Just make sure you empty them first.
- Shoes. Women flock round shoes at car boots. Even scruffy ones seem to sell. Polish them first for added temptation, and expect to get £2-£3 for a pair. I saw someone selling used Crocs at £10 a pair but too high a price means they'll be walking back home. If you have designer shoes, sell them on eBay instead for maximum profit.
- Belts and accessories. You might be bored with them, but others will love them.
- Costume jewellery. There are horror stories of good jewellery being accidentally mixed up with base metal, so double check first. If it has a hallmark and you're not sure where you got it, or if it's worth anything, get it valued first. You could be giving away a fortune otherwise (see p62).
- Videos. Now that most people have swapped from watching films on video recorders to DVDs, sell your old prerecorded videos whilst people still have the machines to watch them on. Though be advised that they now fetch as little as 20p at most boot sales. But it could quickly add up, especially as, pretty soon, they'll be worthless.
- Cassettes and records. A ready market of music-lovers will appreciate your old format music.
- CDs. Get some of your money back if you no longer enjoy your old taste in music. Someone might want your old Steps CDs.
- Computer games. Once you've mastered the game, let someone else enjoy it and get money to buy new ones.

- Furniture. Depending on the size of your car or van, clear out your old tables and chairs when revamping your home, or sell unwanted garden furniture when you get the latest goods.
- Animal accessories. Has your hamster had an upgrade or your dog gone? Sell their old accessories to someone who needs them, and get rid of painful reminders. Even chewed dog beds sell (possibly because other people don't think of hygiene!).
- Old oversized bottles. Huge display bottles sell at car boots. Make money instead of just recycling them.
- Plants. Buy seed packets for under £2, germinate them and sell the young plants for 75p-£1.50, depending on variety. I paid £1.99 for a package of courgette seeds and the plants sold for £1 each. I had 22 of them so that's a good profit for a bit of compost, sun and water. I also buy plants at car boots as they're so much cheaper than at garden centres, and often better quality.

You know you're never going to wear them again, so sell your old shoes and release the money to buy some more.

- Fishing tackle. Specialist dealers in fishing tackle and accessories seem to do very well at car boots, even inland ones. Check with the organiser that you're allowed to sell them first, in case they already have a regular or don't allow new goods to be sold. Print out cards

They were once 'must-have' toys, but Rubik's Cubes and spin-offs have had their fun without crossing over into the collectable world, because so many of them were made. The exceptions are the Royal Wedding and advertising cubes. Clear out your cupboards and swap unwanted goods for cash.

for repeat business.

- Tools are hugely popular. Even rusty spanners seem to hold appeal, and some sellers just put a tarpaulin on the ground and spread (dump) their tools over them for their ready market.

Protect your interests

Not certain if your old records, jewellery or china and glass are worth anything? Check them out at your local auction house before selling them or you could be giving away a fortune.

Auctioneers will value your goods for free (as long as you don't go every week), but a dealer will either charge for a valuation or, if valuing with the potential to buy, could rip you off. A simple rule is never to sell to the person who values your belongings, as they won't have your interest in mind, no matter how honest they are. If it's worth £100, they won't give you £100, as they need to make a profit to pay their own bills.

New goods

Some organisers ban new-goods' vendors and market traders from their car boot. The rules on new goods are a bit more lax, but they don't want traders. If you have one or two new bits, such as unwanted presents amongst your other goods, that's fine. Just don't sell virtually all new goods without checking with the organiser first, or you could waste your pitch rent, petrol and time.

CHAPTER 6

WHAT YOU CAN'T SELL

TRADING Standards have issued a leaflet advising people to be careful about what they sell at car boots. If in doubt, ring your local Trading Standards office for details. I'm not publishing details here because they vary per region, especially in areas where you're expected to register if you're going to be a professional car booter (see p113).

There are different reasons for my 'avoid the following' list. Some goods are illegal to sell, others you need to have a licence and some could have serious repercussions if they are faulty. You could get fined or imprisoned for some, or feel responsible if others go wrong. Some goods are also confiscated on sight, meaning you lose any money you have invested in buying them. Just look after your own interests by protecting others.

To avoid trouble or breaking the law, do not sell the following at car boots unless, in some cases, you have a licence to do so:

- Stolen goods. Even if bought unwittingly, the police will hold you responsible if you're caught selling stolen goods. Be very careful of selling on cheap, boxed DVD players etc. bought in bulk at car boots. If the original seller can't prove they're legitimate, neither can you. Keep all receipts.
- Pirate computer games, computer software, DVDs or CDs.
- Cigarettes and other tobacco. Not just illegal imports.
- Guns. These include replica and BB (ball-bearing) guns. In the wrong hands, such as children, these can cause serious damage, including blindness – as they discovered at my local car boot.
- Alcohol. Even 'miniatures' are in the questionable grey area.
- Illegal goods (e.g. drugs). This is not just common sense. Police, Trading Standards and Customs officers are regular visitors to car boots, often going undercover.

- Knives as weapons. But you can sell cutlery and penknives. If in doubt, and you're hoping to sell old military knives, just speak to the organiser before travelling to the car boot.
- Swords. Even collectable military swords, unless you've spoken to the organiser first.
- Oil or paraffin heaters. Strictly speaking, there is rarely an outright ban on these, but they are often checked by Trading Standards and faulty ones are confiscated. With the risk to buyers so high, it's best to take unwanted ones to your local dump.
- Toys with sharp edges.

Car boot tips

I've actually seen puppies sold at car boots. Whilst often adorable, you shouldn't be tempted to buy them, as they could be puppy farm dogs which come with a variety of health problems. The vets' bills are huge. I had a couple of rescued puppy farm breeding bitches and know just how heart-breaking their frequent health and emotional problems can be. Only buy from proper sources or go to an animal rescue home after the car boot.

- Cycle helmets or riding hats which have had a knock or two.
- Cycles or prams with bad brakes or steering.
- Children's car seats with wear or tear.
- Sofas or soft furnished chairs with no 'fire retardant' labels.
- Electrical goods with frayed cords. Cut off any old cords or plugs. Some car boots don't allow any electrical goods to be sold, but most are fairly lax. Just don't sell any which you know to be dangerous. It does happen and you could be found liable.
- Food and drink. This is a relatively new rule due to Health and Safety reasons and most organisers request that their car booters don't sell any. But as you've seen, this is not always adhered to. Personally, I wouldn't buy or sell food at a car boot as you don't know how it's been stored.
- Out-of-date food. The Trading Standards departments advise people against buying or selling this. There are plenty of market traders who ignore this advice, but Trading Standards can confiscate this type of stock without financial redress.
- Animals. Whilst not all organisers think to ban the selling of live animals, car boots are not the places to do so. You never know who will buy them, or why, and some animals require a licence for sellers, especially exotic animals.
- Pornography. It depends on the organiser, but remember that these are family events and not the place for homemade porn or hard-core DVDs. You could also lose buyers who are turned off by seeing homemade porn on a stall.
- It is illegal to sell both in this country. If selling soft-core DVDs, don't put them where kids can see them. People do sell them, but the organisers have the right to ask them to be put away or even ask the seller to leave.
- Market traders. Ask about selling your goods before the event so you don't get turned away or asked to pack up and leave.

Maximise your profits by making it easy for your buyers to see what's on offer. This pitch shows exactly what not to do. Display books the same way round so their spines are easy to read and keep similar goods together to attract buyers.

CHAPTER 7

ON THE DAY

PACK the car if you haven't done so the night before, and don't forget to use the checklist on p121 so you don't miss out anything important. Trust me, even experienced car booters forget things such as chairs, which is why I always pack an extra one.

Don't forget to have your tables and chairs packed where you can get them out first, not right at the back or under all of your boxes, as first-time car booters are wont to do. Leave enough room down the side of the car to slide a table. If you don't already know how, read the manual to see how your rear seats fold down. This opens up the boot into a much better storage area so you can take extra goods. A lot of people have never done this before their first car boot or when moving house. You normally don't need to, but take advantage of the extra capacity to fit in as much as possible. The more goods you have with you, the larger your potential profit margin. Just remember, you do have to unpack it all, but hopefully, won't have to take it back home with you again.

Print out the directions if you don't know the venue and are travelling alone so can't map read easily. I use the AA's route planner (www.theaa.com), which tells me exactly where to turn, and then draw a basic version of it – e.g. ':: r (right at traffic lights), O l (left at roundabout)'. That's why I rarely get lost – something which I do frequently without my basic maps.

Before I leave, I make sure that I eat breakfast. I don't always eat first thing, but it helps to build up strength when stalling out. I avoid coffee, and I go to the loo before travelling in my efforts to avoid the car boot facilities. My frozen water bottle comes out of the freezer, sandwiches are made the night before (or bought from supermarkets) and I'm almost ready to go. Finally, I get out the exact money for the pitch rent. This saves time, especially if I think there are going to be queues of sellers. Then it's off.

Rain check

If it's been raining, check the organiser's website (if they have one) to see if it's still on. Otherwise, at the crack of dawn, make a telephone check-call before travelling a long distance. For local car boots which are in fields, use your common sense to save a wasted trip. Would you buy from soggy wet fields where your car might get stuck in the mud and be drenched – as will everything that's for sale? I wouldn't.

Parking tricks

I always arrive early, before the gates open, to have a good position. Some regulars get set spaces, including ends of rows. Always try to get the end of a row, so you have that corner space for displaying stock, no one misses you out and you can leave easily.

Never drive right up to the car in front once you're in place, as they need to use their boot and you all want as much space as possible.

I also immediately open my car boot and stand in front of it so the car behind me gives me the space I need for access and a little bit extra. Then, if there isn't a car already next to me, I open the front passenger door and start taking things out, or just stand in front of it, so the car parking next to me isn't virtually touching my car. It's surprising how many people will park as though in a supermarket car park. You need access to all of your doors if, like me, you've crammed your car with lots of items and need room to get them out.

Getting started

First, get out your chairs and table. Set them up so the table is fully secure. If you're not used to car boots, it's easy not to extend the legs fully. So, to ensure the table is fully supported, click fully into place. Set the chairs behind, and use them to rest the boxes on for easy unloading. That way, you don't block your own stall.

Get your notebook and pen ready and then put the calculator in your pocket. After that, you're ready to start unpacking.

CHAPTER 8

UNPACKING

THIS is a minefield for the unwary, even experienced antique dealers. And first-time car booters could be surprised with just how aggressive some buyers can be. Don't be afraid to ask them to wait, and stress that you have some great things they might be interested in. They want to hear that you've got china and glass etc. If they ask about collectables, plead ignorance, saying you're just not sure as you're clearing your house (unless you're a dealer and they know you). That way, they'll be drooling. Don't let them take things

Take advantage of the space on offer to display goods attractively but practically. Make sure there's room for buyers to try out chairs and that they can get close to your stall without tripping over anything.

out of your car, but it's up to you if you want them to start going through your boxes before they're unpacked. I prefer not to, but that's just me. I have years' experience of unpacking in busy conditions, and know it's important not to take too long getting everything out. But it's personal preference. There's no right or wrong way, so do what feels right for you.

I never use a cloth on my stall. Some people do because it looks pretty, but it also looks too professional – just the image you don't want to send out. They also lift up in the wind and knock breakables off the corners or the front of the stall. Ikea sell some tablecloth magnets which are cool, but relatively easy to knock off by accident. I use them on my dining table and, at around £4, it's worth investing in a box of four in case you want to use a cloth on your table – a good option if it's scruffy or covered in wallpaper paste or paint.

WHERE TO START

Leave clothes and books until last, unless already packed in easy-display boxes. You need to bring out the collectables or records first. Unpack boxes, saving the wrapping and putting it back in the box. Do it quickly but, conversely, don't rush or you could break something and get flustered. Just put it out. Realistically, you'll have packed like with like (e.g. kitchen goods together) which makes it easier for unpacking.

Stop to serve, but you can still carry on unpacking if they're just asking questions. Don't forget to make eye contact, so they feel you're paying attention. It generally costs more to get into car boots early, as these are serious buyers after bargains. They have money to spend, so get selling.

When you've finished unpacking, start tidying. Make it look more organised after you've taken everything out, so you don't waste crucial selling time faffing about. Being pretty is good, but not vital at car boots when compared to antiques fairs or craft shows. You don't want to look professional but do want everything to be seen. It's so much easier if the books and CDs come in boxes with the spines face up so people can read them with ease, and they're not sprawled all over the stall.

If selling clothes, start hanging them up once everything is on

Take tarpaulin or waterproof cloths to display goods such as tools which won't break if they fall over. Tools sell very well at car boots, so empty out your toolboxes and see what you haven't used for years, then sell it.

display. Get out first and tidy later for maximum sales.

Have bags and wrapping handy in your boot, or on the spare chair if necessary (but expect to move them for buyers). Have a bag or purse of coins in your pocket or bum bag, then wrap and pack fast and count the money. Don't forget to write sales in your notebook.

CHAPTER 9
SELLING TIPS AND HAGGLING

'PRICE to sell – you'll sell more that way.'

Just relax. This is not life or death, but it can feel overly hectic at your first car boot. Dealers will try to bully you, but just ignore them, smile and be polite. That'll be the case with your first or second car boot. After that, it's a breeze and you'll enjoy it. You will even find the first half hour of the car boot an absolute buzz. I do, and I hated my first car boot because I didn't know what to expect from some of the buyers. You do. Just stand firm, don't let them take things out of your car without permission, and then everything will run smoothly.

HOW TO SELL AT CAR BOOTS

Price is one of the biggest components of successful selling. Even if you're dealing to make a profit or a living, price to sell. You'll sell more, release capital and be able to invest in other goods. Or, if selling to clear space, you'll not only do so, but also make money faster with the right prices.

Know what you want but be prepared to be flexible – within reason. Yes, some buyers, especially dealers, will try to get a bigger discount than you want to offer, but consider each case on its merits. Don't just say 'no' or you won't sell as many goods, make as much money, or even enjoy the experience. And if you want to be a regular, you need to start building up your loyal customer base from your first boot sale.

Alternatively, if you're just doing one or two boots to clear goods, make it as enjoyable an experience as possible. Car boots are fun once you get the hang of them. The vast majority of customers are normal people who just want what you're selling, not necessarily to make a profit but because they like them. But, like everyone – like you – they want to feel that they not only haven't paid over the odds, but have got a bargain. And that's down to you.

SELLING TIPS

I love buying and selling because it's friendly and fun. You get to talk to people and make them happy, whilst you're taking their money off them. That can't be a bad way to earn a living, or extra income. However, you have to realise that not everything will sell itself. Sometimes, you have to work a bit harder, or lower prices that bit further than you'd hoped. And there are easy ways to do this:
• Be friendly, make the person want to buy from you.
• Be willing to haggle and price your goods with this in mind, if

Offer discounts to encourage people to buy more unwanted goods. And display CDs, DVDs, computer games, videos and books spine-up for easy sales.

possible. An extra pound on goods over £6, allows an easy pain-free discount.

- Group similar goods together so the buyers won't have to work to find what they want. You'll sell more that way.
- Display books, CDs and DVDs spine-side up and all facing the same way for easy reading and bigger sales.
- Don't make piles of goods too high. People won't want to lift them or have to move too much and you'll lose sales or risk broken goods.
- Clean your goods before you pack them, so they're more fresh-looking and appealing when you unpack them at the car boot.
- Check any labels to ensure they are legible or are still on the goods. If not, write new ones using the spare labels in your car boot supplies. If it was raining at your last car boot and you didn't remember to change them before, there might be a few new ones needed. Try not to have everything labelled, or you'll look too professional and you could deter 'dealer' buyers.
- If people are buying more than five or 10 of the same goods, (e.g. books or greetings cards), you might want to have a set discount, at least in your mind, so the buyers feel they should be purchasing more for that extra money off. It really does work and is the 'buy two, get one free' philosophy.
- Ask if they want something else, especially if there's something similar on the stall. No big sell, just, 'Did you see this one?' It gives them options without invading their space.
- If you're a regular, or going to be, let them know that you'll be back with similar goods. People will start looking out for you and you'll get regular buyers that way. Don't start buying goods just for them, because they might not turn up or be able to find you (there are no set pitches at car boots) and you could be lumbered with hard-to-sell goods.
- Be welcoming. I was buying a lot of goods from one stall and the novice seller complained, saying she wished I hadn't come because I wanted so many things and she had to pack them all. I ended up asking for a discount when I wouldn't normally – the goods were very cheap, offered great profit margins, and I was buying things for a photo-shoot, so wasn't even using my own money. I ended up never wanting to buy from her again. If you are rude to people, they won't want to help you in return and that means you'll lose money and potential sales.

How not to sell

There are ways to deter buyers, even keen ones, and you might not even realise you're doing it. Don't:

- Be aggressive. Give the buyers space.
- Refuse to haggle. Let them feel they're winning and you'll get their money.
- Show off your knowledge. They want to feel that they've taken advantage of your ignorance. Let them. You'll take their money which is all that matters.
- Follow people when they leave your stall, still trying to sell goods. It's a common mistake and very embarrassing. They won't even look at your stall again before they leave, so you'll lose second-look sales.

Haggling

Expect to haggle. Not all buyers will ask, but most will expect some form of discounts – even on goods under £1. It's part of the car boot 'game', if I must call it that. Just do it, know what you want, but be prepared to let some goods go for a bit less than you'd like You'll make it up on other items where no discount is given at all. Be friendly, smile, and treat the buyer as a friend – not overly so, but just chatter. No aggression, no outright refusal, at least initially.

You won't sell everything. You might be selling it for more than the buyer genuinely wants to pay, but don't get caught up in macho haggling where it almost becomes a matter of honour. Use phrases like, 'I'm afraid I can't, but…' – the but showing flexibility. They'll get a discount – maybe not as high as they want – but you're willing to try. Then it's up to them.

You can't force them to pay what you want, but try getting them to the stage when they want to buy because the price is good, you're friendly and they want it. All or a combination of these, and you've got their money. If not, just let it go. There are always other buyers. But always accept reasonable offers so you're not stuck with goods at car boots. It could be raining next week.

GENERAL ADVICE AND WARNINGS

C AR BOOTS are a very good way to earn money. You don't have
to work hard, carry goods into a venue, drive far (unless you
choose to) or be stuck in a hall and miss the best days of the
summer or work a full day. They're great, especially if you follow the
basic principles of car booting:

- Sort out your goods beforehand –it's what professional car booters
  do. First or second-timers don't think about it and then get caught
  out.
- Be prepared (change, bags, packing, chairs, tables etc.).
- Know where you're going, so you don't get lost en route. This is
  more common than you'd think if you don't know the area.
- Go with the right mindset. Be prepared to haggle and enjoy the day.
  It's not hard work, even if it is your living or essential extra income.
- Arrive early for the best pitch. The later you are, the smaller the size
  of your pitch if the organisers are worried about fitting all the sellers
  in. Not everyone looks all the way round, especially at the rambling
  events, but they always cover all of the first couple of rows.
- Be friendly. You'll get more sales and bigger profits that way, as well
  as potential regulars. It also makes the day even more enjoyable.
- Talk to your neighbouring stalls. Find out where else they stand. Are
  there any issues you should be aware of at that car boot? These
  could include difficulty leaving, grumpy organiser, bad food,
  disgusting toilets, only one toilet that locks (and which one does) etc.
- Look at what the stalls around you are selling. If you buy from
  neighbouring stalls, don't sell the goods that day for a profit or
  you'll antagonise them. That's not what you want if you need them
  to watch your stall when going to the toilet or you need to buy food
  or drink.
- If leaving your stall to use the facilities, always ask your neighbours

to watch it for you. They'll also let would-be buyers know that you won't be long so, hopefully, you won't lose sales.

- Never use a handbag at car boots as it could get stolen if you put it down – even if you think you've hidden it in your open car boot.
- Make sure you have enough change.
- Be willing to haggle. There's no such thing as a set price at car boots.
- Don't forget to drink, wear sun cream and a hat (if necessary) during summer car boots.
- Layer up to cope with the different temperatures during the day.
- Make a note of every sale, so you have records to show the tax man.
- Register with Trading Standards in areas where it's compulsory for traders or regular car booters to be certified (see p113).

Car boot warnings

This isn't just about looking after your money and not leaving it where it can get stolen.

Car boot registration

With compulsory registration for regular car booters in some areas (see p113), it's essential that you keep the right records and carry your certificate with you to avoid being fined. If you don't want to get involved, just sell in the nearest registration-free area, but don't risk being a regular in areas where you have to register or you could get fined or have goods confiscated.

Police and Trading Standards

Don't waste money by knowingly buying stolen goods or forbidden items to sell at car boots (or anywhere else, for that matter). If Trading Standards or the police catch you – and they do visit car boots on a regular basis – not only will the goods be confiscated, but you could also be prosecuted. Is a £2 pirate computer software programme, CD or DVD, or pack of illegally imported cigarettes, really worth it?

There are other goods which are regularly checked for Health and Safety reasons – toys with sharp corners, kids' bikes, cycle helmets, prams and car seats. Oil and paraffin heaters are renowned for causing accidents which is why, ideally, they shouldn't be sold at car boots. These are also checked by Trading Standards trying to avoid potentially lethal goods from being sold. If in doubt, don't sell anything which you don't trust to be safe. Dispose of it safely at your local tip/dump instead.

Be careful what toys you buy or sell at car boots. Ensure that they're child-friendly, so no sharp corners. Bikes must be safe to ride. And know what you're selling. This 50p Anne Geddes doll is a future collectable or worth £5 now on eBay.

CHAPTER 11

PACKING UP

WHEN do car boot sales end? Generally, a lot earlier than advertised, but some organisers have unofficial agreements for the earliest acceptable leaving time and you need to be aware of this. Don't ask the organisers, because they'll want you to stay until the very end. Ask the regulars, and also watch when other sellers start packing. The organisers need it to be as close to the advertised time as possible, especially if they're still taking entrance fees on the gate.

I aim to be home by about 1pm, and generally start to leave between 11am-noon, depending on the venue and how well I'm doing. Obviously, if there are still buyers about, I stay. If it's virtually bereft of trade, why stay? And that's if it's not raining. The rain tends to signal the end of the event, with the exception of indoor or partly indoor venues. Light showers, or a bit of drizzle, are watched with unease, but the conversation during many car boots is weather-related. We watch the skies for warnings all day and, when it starts getting too heavy to trade, we go home, no matter what the time is. But don't leave too early if the weather's fine or you'll miss out on profitable sales.

PACKING

I start putting clothes and books in the car first, regardless of the weather. But if it is raining, these should certainly be the priority, together with any other paper-type goods and electrics. Clothes and books will sell more slowly at the end of the fair than household goods and collectables. I pack these last, using the extra newspaper I brought with me. It is true: you never have as much usable wrapping at the end of the sale as when you unpacked. Pack safely to avoid breakages, no matter what the weather. Load the car – leaving enough room to slip the table down the side (if that's how you pack). Double-check you haven't left anything behind. Don't forget to do your final tally so you can see how well you did.

AT HOME

You've probably had to queue to get out. It shouldn't take that long at most car boots, especially if not everyone leaves together. If it was raining at the car boot or when you were packing, change any wet or ink-run labels and soggy paper and replace with dry paper. Soggy boxes will fall apart, so change them now. Go through the car boot checklist and make a note of anything which needs replenishing, including change, and put the car boot change away for next time. Now you're all set for your next car boot.

Enjoy it – and make money!

CHAPTER 12

INTERNET CAR BOOTS

I NTERNET car boots sound like a good idea in theory, but the reality is that they simply cannot compete with eBay. Whilst writing this book, I looked at many of them, and came to the same conclusions:

- I personally would never sell at an internet car boot.
- I'd never buy from one either.
- eBay is so much better.

And that's the trouble. It's not just me, but the wealth of internet car boot sites on offer is not matched by their goods. Some of them didn't even have a single item for sale, despite free listings being offered as an incentive.

ADVANTAGES OF INTERNET CAR BOOTS

When eBay started, no one knew just how successful it would become. But it means buying and selling without stall rent, petrol, or even having to leave the house. If one of my favourite car boots was on but it was raining so hard that I didn't fancy going, that's when internet car boots should come into their own:

- Never rained off.
- Year-round.
- No petrol costs.
- On all of the time, not dependent on set days and hours like traditional car boots.
- Don't have to take time off work or away from the family to buy or sell.
- Set prices so you don't have to wait for an auction to end or miss out on something if you get outbid.
- Some sites and sellers allow haggling, but not all.
- Cheaper costs than eBay. Many even offer free listings.

DISADVANTAGES OF INTERNET CAR BOOTS

Selling unwanted goods has certainly worked for eBay, but that's partly because of the goods on offer. I have yet to see a single internet car boot I'd recommend. One or two (not listed here) even looked incredibly dodgy and I wouldn't risk giving them my details, even if they were advertising something worth buying. But the disadvantages, to me, outweigh the positives:

- The prices are far higher than normal car boots.
- Unlike a car boot, you can't inspect the goods and have to rely on the descriptions.
- There are some surprisingly high P&P costs.
- Unlike a car boot, you have to wait for the goods to arrive.
- Not all sites or sellers allow haggling, so over-priced goods don't have the discount potential of a traditional car boot.
- Many don't have photos, so you can't see what's on offer or its condition.
- Some don't even have prices, but ask for 'offers' even if you can't see what they're selling.
- It is currently an unpopular medium, so there are few potential sellers.
- A dearth of goods on offer drives away would-be buyers who don't feel the need to keep looking (unlike eBay).
- They are not taken seriously by most car booters, so word of mouth is lacking.
- There is a lack of confidence in the market.
- They just can't compete with eBay and its massive community and advertising budget.

But that's just my opinion. Why not decide for yourself?

INTERNET CAR BOOTS

These are some of the internet car boots currently operating. I have not tried any, and do not personally recommend buying or selling through them until they improve, but you might want to be there almost at the beginning. Some of those listed are at an early stage or during the four-week period in which I watched them, have yet to offer a single item

for sale. But things may change, so check them out for yourself:
    www.iBootsale.co.uk – probably the best online car boot
    www.bitsnbobs.co.uk
    www.carboot.info
    www.virtualcarboot.co.uk
    www.online-boot-sale.com
    www.karbootsale.co.uk
    www.giantcarboot.co.uk
    www.ukfayres.co.uk

TAX MATTERS

YOU NEED to keep a record of your sales, whether you're a regular car booter or antique dealer, even if it's not a career, but an extra income. This is because the tax office will charge you if you get caught and, if you're really unlucky, they'll also start looking back at previous years. They do visit antiques fairs and car boots, collecting details and following them up afterwards. Most people just assume car boots are cash-in-hand affairs, so they don't need to keep records. They're wrong. Just protect your interests by registering your extra income.

Ring your local tax office for advice on self-employment and keep a record of everything you buy to sell at car boots, as well as what you sell. That way, you can show what your taxable profits are (not the same as your takings which are higher). Don't forget to make a note of pitch fees, as these are tax deductible. Food and drink isn't. Petrol for stalling out isn't tax deductible, whilst it is for buying stock. Make a note of all of your mileage for this reason, so you don't pay more tax than you should. But ask your accountant or your local tax office (the number is in your phone directory) for advice and keep records.

WHAT'S TAX DEDUCTIBLE?

- Your stock. Keeping records ensures that you don't pay too much tax.
- Petrol for buying stock. But not for selling, as that counts as driving to a place of work.
- Pitch fees. Speak to the organisers when it's quiet, (not on arrival when you're paying and there is a huge queue behind you), and get a receipt. Even take your own receipt book with you, in case they don't have one.
- Items needed to keep paperwork e.g. receipt book and notebooks to record sales.

- Labels and bags.
- Calculators.
- Tables, cloths and chairs bought for car booting.
- Any extras incurred by car booting, except food and drink, which is not tax deductible.
- Phone calls made to organisers or potential buyers.
- If you buy a mobile specifically for the business, the phone, any rental and any calls are tax deductible. Just remember to keep your phone bills.
- This book is tax deductible if you're buying it to help you make a profit from car booting.
- If you're registered (see p113), your paperwork will be very similar, but in many areas you are expected to keep separate records from your normal tax affairs, so they can be inspected when needed. Keep clear books explaining every expense and stock purchase, so you can answer questions if need be.
- Get your tax return in early, pay what you need, and don't worry about it. Filling in a tax return is quick and easy if you keep your figures updated regularly. I do mine on the day when selling, so I know exactly what I've bought and sold. I also keep a track of everything I've had to buy for business use, so that when it's time to fill in the return, I don't have to get stressed out trying to find pieces of paper or old receipts. It's all in one place, in a file and ready for inspection should I need it. Just keep good paperwork. And if you don't think the seller will give you a receipt, make a note of your own purchases at the time, so you know exactly what your profit is when you sell the goods. No one likes to pay tax but what you're really paying for is peace of mind. I've seen too many raids at antiques fairs and centres to think you can evade the taxman for long.

INFORMATION AND DIRECTORY

Discover what's on, where and when in the car boot directory – over 815 events listed.

DIRECTORY OF CAR BOOT SALES

NEW CAR boots start up all the time. There are signs on the road and ads in the local press signalling new events. Others close down unexpectedly and, apart from the indoor car boots, all are susceptible to the weather. Ring the organiser the day before the event if intending to travel long distance to check that the car boot is still on as many are weather dependent. And don't forget to ask if they have any other events, as some organisers will run several car boots, sometimes even on the same day in the same county. So, if you have time, you can do two or more car boots in one day.

Check your local press around Bank Holidays for special car boots. Charities and stately homes tend to use these days for one-off events which won't be listed here. I've also listed flea markets, as they have many of the same components and sellers as car boots. These are catagorised as such so you know what to expect.

Please note: the times listed are the official start and end times. Speak to the organisers for more accurate details. And don't expect to see many – if any – stalls at the stated finish time. Most car booters will have left by then.

Days listed are often seasonal (March/April-October). Ask the organiser the day before the event or check the bi-monthly listings in *Car Boot and Fairs Calendar* (available from all medium-large car boots or see p221 for details).

FOOD TRADERS

Most organisers already have regular concession stalls and others do not allow any food to be sold without prior permission. If in doubt, ring the organiser before travelling if you are a food trader.

Note: 'no food' or 'no food traders' denotes that no food is allowed to be sold; it doesn't mean no food is available at the car boot.

ABERDEENSHIRE

To be a regular seller at car boots in this county (and the whole of Scotland), you need to register with Trading Standards (see p113 for more details)

Hard-standing Indoor and Outdoor Car Boot
Thainstone Centre, off A96
INVERURIE
Sundays, 8am-4pm
Separate area for new goods/market traders
01467 623700

ANGLESEY

Treetops Country Club, Bwlch Lane
BENLLECH
Saturdays, 8am
01248 853075, 01248 853146

Mona Car Boot, Opposite Airfield, A5
Nr GWALCHMAI, LLANGEFNI
Sundays (year-round), 6am
01407 840179

ANGUS

To be a regular seller at car boots in this county (and the whole of Scotland), you need to register with Trading Standards (see p113 for more details)

Seaton Park Football Park
ARBROATH
Sundays (March-November), 9.30am
email: Claireyeoman01@hotmail.co.uk

AVON

See Bristol or Somerset

AYRSHIRE

To be a regular seller at car boots in this county (and the whole of Scotland), you need to register with Trading Standards (see p113 for more details)

Indoor and Outdoor Hard-standing Car Boot & Market
Ayr Racecourse
AYR
Sundays (year-round), 9.30am-4pm
Food traders to speak to the organisers in advance
Spook Erections, 01386 765403
www.spookerection.com/sco_ayr.php

BEDFORDSHIRE

Afternoon Car Boot
Bedford Town Football Club, Meadow Lane
CARDINGTON, BEDFORD
Sundays (monthly), 10.30-2pm,
Buyers from 12pm
01234 381213

G M Growers, Hitchin Rd
UPPER CALDECOTE, BIGGLESWADE
Sundays, 6am (from late-March-December)
Market traders should speak to the organisers in advance in case of restrictions. No plants or flowers allowed because of the farm shop next door
077 8926 8964 / www.carbootmarket.com

Shortmead Car Boot
Shortmead St
BIGGLESWADE
Sundays (July-October), 6am
No number listed

Billington Rd, Stanbridge
BILLINGTON, Nr LEIGHTON BUZZARD
Thursdays, 7am-1pm
Sundays, 9am-1pm
Bank Holiday Mondays, 6am-1pm
078 3128 4793

The Old Brickworks,
Marston Rd
LIDLINGTON
Sunday and Bank Holiday Mondays (April-October), 11am, buyers from 1pm
Note: *At the time of writing, the event is for sale so the listed number might have changed*
01525 405598 / www.lidlingtoncarboot.tk

Stondonbury Reuse Boot
Shillington Rd
LOWER STONDON
Sundays (from Easter Sunday-October), 10am
Buyers from 12pm
*No market traders or new goods. No unpacking
before 10am*
079 8420 6698 / www.stondon-carboot.co.uk

Afternoon Car Boot
Flitton Rd, nr Flitwick
PULLOXHILL
Sundays (May-September), 10am
Buyers from 11am
077 8926 8964 / www.carbootmarket.com

BERKSHIRE

High St, opp Barclays Bank
ASCOT
Bank Holiday Mondays, 7am-1.30pm
Greatcarboots, 079 3153 9282

Racecourse Car Parks
ASCOT
Sundays, 6am, buyers from 7am
No new goods
No number listed

Garth Hill Secondary School, Priestwood
BRACKNELL
Sunday (April-September), 6am
Buyers from 7.30am
No number listed

Big Ron's Car Boot
Abbey Rugby Field, Peppard Rd (B481)
EMMER GREEN
Sundays, 11am, buyers from 12pm
01296 713 7717

Giant Car Boot/Afternoon Car Boot
Bath Rd (Junc 7, M4)
MAIDENHEAD / TAPLOW
Sundays, Good Friday and Bank Holiday
Mondays (late March-early winter), 10am-5pm,
buyers from 10.30am, reduced entry fee after
1pm
*Vans welcome. Changes from Sundays to Bank
Holiday Mondays where necessary*
079 5648 6448 / www.giantcarboot.co.uk

Burghclere Car Boot
The Clere School, Earlstone Common
BURGHCLERE, NEWBURY
One Sunday a year in June (at the time of
writing), 10am
Burghclere Pre-school, 01635 276000

Reading Big Car Boot
Reading Showground, Reading Rd (A33),
Swallowfield Bypass
SWALLOWFIELD, READING
Sundays and Bank Holiday Mondays, 7am-
2pm, reduced entry fees for buyers after 8am
Thames Valley Fairs, 01491 832196

Pangbourne Primary School, Reading Rd
(A329)
PANGBOURNE, READING
2nd Sunday of every month (April-September),
9am
01189 613591

Woodley Table Top and Car Boot
Woodley Town Centre
WOODLEY, READING
Last Sunday of every month, 7.30am-12.30pm
Buyers from 8am
League of Friends of the Royal Berks, 0118
9216920

Giant Car Boot & Market
Whitehouse Farm, Silchester Rd
TADLEY
Sundays, 6am-1pm
Hughmark, 0118 945 1799

Wokingham Big Car Boot
Cantley Park, Twyford Rd
WOKINGHAM
August Bank Holiday Monday, 7am
Buyers from 8am
Thames Valley Fairs, 01491 832196

BORDERS

See Scottish Borders

*To be a regular seller at car boots in this
county (and the whole of Scotland), you
need to register with Trading Standards
(see p113 for more details)*

BRIDGEND

See Glamorganshire

BRISTOL

Beesmoor Rd Playing Field, Beesmoor Rd
FRAMPTON COTTERELL, BRISTOL
Sundays (May-August), 8am, buyers from 9am
01454 852157

Cog Mill Car Boot
Cog Mill Farm, Old Bristol Rd (B4058)
FRAMPTON COTTERELL, BRISTOL
Saturdays (April-September), 7am
Buyers from 8.30am
Held in field by main road
01454 772228

Memorial Rd
HANHAM, BRISTOL
Saturdays and Sundays (from July), 7am
No number listed

Community Centre, Longwell Green
BRISTOL
Bank Holiday Mondays, 10am-1pm
Set up from 8.30am
0117 932 3737

Indoor Fleamarket
Bristol BAWA, Southmead Rd, Filton
BRISTOL
Sundays, 9.30am-3.30pm
Felix Fairs, 01275 842480

BUCKINGHAMSHIRE

Car Boot
Stablebridge Rd, (off A41)
ASTON CLINTON, AYLESBURY
Sundays and Bank Holiday Mondays (April-
October), 11am
James Bone, 01296 614749

Bric-a-brac Market
Market Square
AYLESBURY
Town & Country, 01952 242019

Afternoon Car Boot
The Meadows, Chinnor Rd, nr West Wycombe
BLEDLOW RIDGE
Sundays (mid-July-October) and Bank Holiday
Mondays, 12.30pm-5pm, buyers from 1pm
Big Bens, 01981 250591
www.bigbenscarboots.co.uk

Outdoor Fleamarket
Old Cattle Pens, nr Museum
BUCKINGHAM
Saturdays, 8am-4pm
01280 816426

Giant Car Boot
Fields by the A40 Roundabout nr Gerrards
Cross (Junc 1, M40)
DENHAM
Saturdays (from late-March-late-autumn), 8am-
3pm, buyers from 8.30am
*It has been known to start earlier – this was my
regular car boot before my house move as it's superb
and full of great buys*
079 4712 1336 / www.giantcarboot.co.uk

Finmere Aerodrome, Bicester to Buckingham
Rd (A421)
FINMERE
Saturdays, 7am, buyers from 7.30am
The Platt Group, 078 5091 2181

Indoor Car Boot
Community Centre, Straight Bit
**FLACKWELL HEATH, (nr HIGH
WYCOMBE)**
Sundays (from November, winter only), 9am
Buyers from 9.30am
Winter indoor car boot, 50+ sellers
079 1236 7671 / www.buckscarboot.co.uk

Afternoon Car Boot
Mumfords Lane, Oxford Rd (off A40)
GERRARDS CROSS
Saturdays (from mid-February), from 1pm
Buyers from 2pm
MD Car Boots, 01753 663656

Guide Dogs Summer Fête and Car Boot
Loughton Sports & Social Club, Linceslade
Grove
LOUGHTON, MILTON KEYNES
1 Saturday in July (annual), 11am

Buyers from 12.30pm
0871 222 3129

National Bowl H7
MILTON KEYNES
Sundays, 6am
077 8926 8964 / www.carbootmarket.com

Bric-a-brac Market
Midsummer Boulevard
MILTON KEYNES
Thursdays, 8am-2pm
Bray Assocs, 01895 639912

Potterspury Giant Car Boot
Behind the Super Sausage (A5)
POTTERSPURY, MILTON KEYNES
Sundays (mid-May-mid-October), 10am
Buyers from 12pm
01908 543008

Afternoon Car Boot
Cowleaze Field, Oxford Rd (A40), nr High
Wycombe
WEST WYCOMBE
Sundays, March-end July, Good Friday,
12.30pm-5pm, buyers from 1pm
Big Bens, 01981 250591
www.bigbenscarboots.co.uk

Agaro Hard-standing Car Boot and Market
Agaro Market, Chruch St
WOLVERTON (nr MILTON KEYNES)
Fridays and Saturdays (year-round), 8am
Buyers from 9am
Market traders should ring to check availability
079 2786 8648

CAMBRIDGESHIRE

Huntingdon Racecourse
BRAMPTON
Sundays and Good Friday
DDF Fairs Ltd, 079 8658 3232

Cambridge Football Club, City Ground
Milton Rd
CAMBRIDGE
Sundays (year-round), 7am
Cambridge City Football Club, 01223 357973

Hard-standing Car Boot
Cowley Rd Park & Ride
CAMBRIDGE
Sundays (year-round), 6.30am-2.30pm
Buyers from 7.30am
S & W, 020 7240 7405

Afternoon Car Boot
Pavilion Ground
DURLINGHAM
Sundays, 2pm
01638 507028 / 079 0008 1817

Market Field, Colins Hill
FORDHAM, nr NEWMARKET
Alternate Sundays (June-October), 7am
078 3635 9502

Chaplins Farm, Cheeky Monkeys,
Babraham Rd
FULBOURN, nr CAMBRIDGE
Sundays (April-October), 7am
Buyers from 7.30am
078 3165 1258

*Hardstanding, Grass, Under-cover and Outdoor
Car Boot*
Oakington Airfield
OAKINGTON
Saturdays (starts March), 9am-3pm
01733 350052 / 077 7622 2074

Focus Youth Centre, Chestnut Ave
PETERBOROUGH
Sundays, 7am, buyers from 8am
079 0053 7340

Hard-standing Car Boot
Wirrina Car Park, Bishops Rd, Eastfield
PETERBOROUGH
Sundays and Bank Holiday Mondays (March-
October), 6am, buyers from 7am
*Entrance has height restrictions, sellers must not
leave before noon*
T.D. Promotions, 01733 763689

Off Cromwell Rd
WISBECH
Wednesdays (indoor only), 4.30pm
Fridays (indoor and outdoor), 4.30pm
Sundays and Bank Holidays (outdoor only),
4.30pm
01945 410013

CARDIFF

See Glamorganshire

CARMARTHENSHIRE

Challenge Supplies, Shands Rd
AMMANFORD
1st Saturday of the month (March-December)
7am, buyers from 8am
01269 842718

Home Start Dinefwr Car Boot
Co-op Car Park, Margaret St
AMMANFORD
One Saturday in June, 8am, buyers from 9am
Note, this might not be an annual event
01269 593853

Indoor and Outdoor Car Boot
Carmarthen Showground
CARMARTHEN
Sundays, 8am-2pm, buyers from 9am
077 8594 8636

CEREDIGION

Pennant Car Boot
Llanon
ABERYSTWYTH
Sundays (March-October), 7am
Buyers from 8am
No number listed

Talsarn Yard (B4337)
LAMPETER
Sundays, (March-October), 7am
Buyers from 9am
079 6649 3580 / www.talsarncarboot.com

CHESHIRE

See also Greater Manchester

Fleamarket
Town Centre Market
ALTRINCHAM
Thursdays, 8am-4pm
0161 929 6881

Moat Hall, Marthall
CHELFORD
Sundays and Bank Holiday Mondays, 8am
01625 861214

Countess of Chester Hospital, Liverpool Rd
Upton
CHESTER
Sundays (March-December), 6am-1pm
No vans allowed
01244 365000

Rugby Club, Tarvin Rd, Vickers Cross
CHESTER
Sundays (May-September), 10am
No number listed

Under-cover Car Boot
Princess St
CONGLETON
Sundays, 7am
077 3952 9225

Rear of Market Hall, Heath St
CREWE
Wednesdays, 9.30am-1pm
01270 537777

Supermarket (formerly Safeway)
CREWE
Sundays, 7am
078 9011 1440

Moat Hall Farm
KNUTSFORD
Sundays (March-December)
077 7465 5917

Adelphi Mill, Bollington
MACCLESFIELD
Sundays (March-June), 8am, buyers from 9am
No number listed

Crewe Vagrants Sports Club, Newcastle Rd
Willaston
NANTWICH
(Sundays (mid-April-end of summer), 8am
No number listed

Neston Cricket Club, Station Rd
PARKGATE
Set Saturdays or Sundays (no pattern, from
May-October), 7.30am-12pm
Buyers from 8.30am

0151 336 2014
www.nestontennis.co.uk/carboots.aspx

Poynton Car Boot & Table Top
Poynton Community Centre, Park Lane
POYNTON, STOCKPORT
3rd Sunday in the month (year-round), 6am
079 7178 4430

Houldsworth Mill Car Boot & Table Top
Houldsworth Mill Shopping Village 2
Houldsworth St
REDDISH, STOCKPORT
Sundays (from May), 8.30am
Buyers from 10am
No number listed

Halton Lea Shopping Centre, Halton Lea
RUNCORN
Sundays (from May), 8am, buyers from 9am
075 1546 8785

Rixton Car Boot
Former Garden Centre, A57 Liverpool Rd,
between Cadishead and Warrington
WARRINGTON
Sundays (from April), 7am, buyers from 7.30am
No number listed

Market Area, Townfield Lane, Winfield
WARRINGTON
Sundays (from May), 7am, buyers from 7.30am
Stockdeal Ltd, 078 3159 0443
www.yourcarbootsale.co.uk

Hard-standing Car Boot
Roll Inn Truck Stop, Tanhouse Lane
WIDNES
Sundays (year-round), 6am
email: Scoucermarc29@aol.com

CLEVELAND

Afternoon Car Boot
Ofca Community Farm
Summerhill Lane
HARTLEPOOL
Saturdays in August, 12.30pm-4pm
Buyers from 1pm
01429 283188

Car Boot & Table Top

The Phoenix Centre, Hindpool Close
Central Estate
HARTLEPOOL
2nd Sunday of every month (year-round)
10am, buyers from 11am
Stalls must be booked in advance
The Phoenix Centre, 01429 284990

Winter Indoor Boro Car Boot
The Southlands Centre, off Ormesby Rd
PRIESTLANDS, MIDDLESBOROUGH
Sundays (November-February), 1pm
Buyers from 2pm
Ad-mire Promotions, 077 5829 5523

Afternoon Car Boot
Redcar Racecourse, West Dyke Rd
REDCAR
Saturdays (year-round), 11am
Buyers from 12.30pm
Also Bank Holidays and Good Friday
No food or drink traders without prior permission
Northern Promotions, 0844 800 3394
www.northernpromotions-fairs.co.uk

Outdoor Boro Car Boot
A171 Middlesborough to Guisborough Rd
UPSALL, MIDDLESBOROUGH
Sundays (March-November), 9am
Buyers from 10.30am
2nd Saturday of every month (from April)
Autojumble, 9am, buyers from 10.30am
Ad-mire Promotions, 077 5829 5523

CLWYD

Market Site, Love Lane
MOLD
Sundays, 7.30am
01352 703110

CONWY

Hotpoint Club, Victoria Drive
LLANDUDNO
Sundays, 8am
No number listed

K4 Car Boot
113, Conway Rd

LLANDUDNO JUNCTION
Sundays (year-round), 7am
Buyers from 8am
01492 582527

Glan-Conwy Strawberry Fields
PENTREFOELAS
Saturdays
01492 581175

CORNWALL

Priory Park Car Park, Town Centre
BODMIN
Sundays (year-round), 7.30am
No number listed

Tregainlands Car Boot
Bodmin / Wadebridge Rd (A389)
BODMIN
Bank Holiday Mondays, 9am
079 7011 8757

Pendeen Charity Car Boot
Stratton, Bude Junction (A39)
BUDE
Sundays (end-April/May-September),
12.30pm, buyers from 1.30pm
078 1466 8567

Afternoon Car Boot
Falmouth Rugby Club, Carrick Rd
FALMOUTH
Fridays (April-November) inc Good Friday,
12pm, buyers from 1pm
No market traders
078 078 078 88 or 077 7951 7749
www.carbootscornwall.co.uk

Frogpool Car Boot
Frogpool
FROGPOOL
Sundays (April-September), 7am
Buyers from 7.30am
No number listed

Hayle Rugby Club, Memorial Park
Marsh Lane
HAYLE
Sundays (year-round), 8am
Buyers from 8.30am
01736 757157 / 01736 753320

Carnebone Car Boot
Falmouth to Heston Rd (A394)
Nr HELSTON
Tuesdays (May-September), 10am
Buyers from 11am
077 6558 1590

Launceston Lions Car Boot
Launceston College Car Park
LAUNCESTON
4th Saturday of every month, 8am
Buyers from 9am
Launceston Lions, No number listed

Liskeard Cricket Club, Recreation Centre
St Cleer Rd
LISKEARD
Fridays (June-September), 4pm
Bank Holiday Mondays, 7.30am
Lieskeard Cricket Club, No number listed

Rapsons Field Car Park
LISKEARD
Sundays (January-April), 9.30am
01503 240104

Sterts Art and Environmental Centre
Upton Cross
LISKEARD
Saturdays (from March), 10.30am
Buyers from 11.30am
01579 362382 / www.sterts.co.uk

Afternoon Car Boot
Shindig Showground, Antron Hill
MABE
Sundays (March-October), 1.30pm
078 078 078 88 / 077 7951 7749
www.carbootscornwall.co.uk

Afternoon Car Boot
Penscawen Lane
Newquay Junction (A30)
MITCHELL
Saturdays (March-October), 12pm
Buyers from 1pm
Bank Holiday Mondays, 9.30am
078 078 078 88 / 077 7951 7749
www.carbootscornwall.co.uk

Car Boot & Market
Circus Field, Morrisons Roundabout
Treloggan Rd

NEWQUAY
Tuesdays (March-October), 12pm
078 078 078 88 / 077 7951 7749
www.carbootscornwall.co.uk

Afternoon Car Boot
Hendra Holiday Park, Treloggan Rd
NEWQUAY
Thursdays (April-October), 12pm
Strictly no arrival before 8am
078 078 078 88 / 077 7951 7749
www.carbootscornwall.co.uk

Indoor Car Boot & Table Top
Newquay WI Hall, Crantock St
NEWQUAY
Wednesdays (March-October), 7.30am-4pm
Buyers from 10am
Advisable to book in advance
01637 859058

Gulval Cricket Club
St Ives Rd, Gulval
PENZANCE
Fridays (June-October), 8.30am
Buyers from 9am
Gulval Cricket Club, no number listed

Penzance & Newlyn Rugby Club,
Alexandra Rd
PENZANCE
Thursdays, 12pm
01736 364044

Car Boot & Market
Off A30 Cambourne/Redruth
POOL
Saturdays and Sundays, 9.30am
Town & Country, 07980 731351

Porthlevan Football Club, Gala Park, Mill Lane
PORTHLEVAN
Thursdays (April-October), 8am
01209 612568

Rosudgeon Football Club
ROSUDGEON
Wednesdays (from Easter-October), 10.30am
Buyers from 11.30am
Rosudgeon Football Club, no number listed

Par, Par Moor Rd
ST AUSTELL

Sundays, 8am
078 1464 7756

Restormel Council Offices (A390)
ST AUSTELL
Sundays, 7.30am
01726 851035

Indoor Afternoon Car Boot
St Paul's Church Hall, Church Rd
CHARLESTOWN
Sundays (year-round), 1pm-4pm
It is advisable to book
Indoor Car Boot, 01726 891860 / 077 4832 5300
www.indoorcarboot.co.uk

Tregorrick Rd, Next to St Austell Rugby Club
ST AUSTELL
Saturdays (April-October), 12pm
Buyers from 1pm
No number listed

Indoor Car Boot & Fleamarket
Alexander Hall, Next to Somerfield
ST BLAZEY
Fridays and Saturdays (year-round) 7.30am
Buyers from 8.30am
It is advisable to book
078 1464 7756

Indoor and Outdoor Car Boot
Providence Farm, Castle An Dinas
ST COLUMB
Sundays, 6am
01637 889143

Indoor Fleamarket
The Guildhall
ST IVES
Wednesdays, 10am-4pm
01736 757625

Sithians Showground
SITHIANS
Wednesdays (April-September), 11.30am
Buyers from 1.30pm
078 078 078 88 / 077 7951 7749
ww.carbootscornwall.co.uk

Allweather Car Boot
Cattle Market, Newquay Rd
TRURO
Saturdays (April-December), 7am

Buyers from 8am
In the event of bad weather, sellers have to unload their goods from their cars to the indoor sheep pens. Strictly no sales before 8am
078 078 078 88 / 077 7951 7749
www.carbootscornwall.co.uk

Royal Cornwall Showground (A39)
WADEBRIDGE
Sundays (March-April), 9am-1pm
Saturdays (July-October), 5pm-9pm
078 078 078 88 / 077 7951 7749
www.carbootscornwall.co.uk

COUNTIES ANTRIM AND DOWN

Belfast is often listed as being in both counties. To avoid confusion, they are listed together

Dunsilly Hard-standing Car Boot
Dunsilly Rd, Ballymena Rd (M2, Junction 1)
DUNSILLY, ANTRIM
Saturdays (year-round), 6am-2pm
Wednesdays (year-round), 5.30pm-dark
02894 463689 / www.dunsillyboot.com

Bangor Academy and Sixth Form College
Gransha Rd
BANGOR
Saturdays (September), 7am
No number listed

Clonmany Community Centre
BELFAST
Saturdays, 12pm
02890 76938/76772

Hillview Retail Park, Crumlin Rd
BELFAST
Saturdays (year-round), 9am
Sundays (year-round), 12pm
Colliers Cre, 02890 241500

Streamvale Car Boot
Streamvale Open Farm, 38, Ballyhanwood Rd
GILNAHIRK, BELFAST
Saturdays (September-October), 9.30am
Charity bootsale. The farm is signposted from the Ulster Hospital
02890 283244 / www.streamvale.com

Hard-standing Car Boot
Dunrod Presbyterian Church
Leathemstown Rd
DUNROD
Last Saturday of the month (March-October), 8am, buyers from 9am
02894 452001

Jim Baker Car Boot
Jim Baker Bowling Stadium, Parkgate
TEMPLEPATRICK
Fridays (April-September), 4.45pm
02894 432937

COUNTY DURHAM

Afternoon Car Boot
Rosemount Rd
SOUTH CHURCH, BISHOP AUCKLAND
Fridays (June-September), 12pm
Buyers from 1pm
079 8984 1374

Afternoon Car Boot
Northbondgate Car Park
Sunday, 12pm, buyers from 1pm
BISHOP AUCKLAND
Noble Promotions, 0191 586 8131
www.noble-promotions.homecall.co.uk

Opposite Batley Cash & Carry, Beamish Rd (A693)
CHESTER LE STREET
Sundays, 7am, buyers from 8am
Noble Promotions, 0191 586 8131
www.noble-promotions.homecall.co.uk

Afternoon Indoor and Outdoor Hard-standing Car Boot
Multi-storey Car Park, Central Avenue, Opposite Police Station
NEWTON AYCLIFFE
Sundays (year-round), 10am
Buyers from 12pm
Indoor height restriction of 6' 5" and outside height restriction of 8' 6"
01325 320319

Afternoon Car Boot
Seaham to Ryhope Coast Rd
SEAHAM

Sundays, 12pm, buyers from 1pm
Noble Promotions, 0191 586 8131
www.noble-promotions.homecall.co.uk

Sedgefield Racecourse, Roman Rd
(Junct 60 A1 (M))
SEDGEFIELD
Thursdays and Bank Holidays, from 10am
Sundays, from 6.30am
DDF Fairs Ltd, 079 8658 3232 / 078 0805 8805

Swan Castle Farm Car Boot
Shotton Colliery (B1280)
SHOTTON COLLIERY
Sundays (April-winter), 12pm
Buyers from 1pm
No dogs apart from guide dogs, no food traders
No number listed

Weardale Open Air Swimming Pool, Front St
Castle Park
STANHOPE
Last Sunday of the month, 10am
01388 528466

Next to Blakeston School, Junction Rd
NORTON, STOCKTON-ON-TEES
Sundays, 11am, buyers from 1pm
No number listed

CUMBRIA

Ambleside Rugby Club
AMBLESIDE
Saturdays and Bank Holiday Mondays
9am-2pm
01539 432252

Barrow Squash Club Car Park, St Georges St
BARROW-IN-FURNESS
Every other Sunday (May-December), 8.30am
077 9352 5253

The Newton Inn, 2-4 Newton Rd
DALTON-IN-FURNESS
Last Sunday of every month (year-round)
12pm, buyers from 1pm
Book and pay in advance
01229 462399

Endmoor Village Hall, Woodside Rd
ENDMOOR, KENDAL
Sundays (March-October), 8am

Booking in advance is recommended
01524 782436

Kendal Rugby Club, Shap Rd
KENDAL
Sundays (April-September), 7.30am
Buyers from 9am
01539 734039

Greenhalgh Car Boot
Junction 3 of the M55
KIRKHAM
Saturdays (April-September), 7am
Can be seen from Junction 3 of the M55
Century Fairs, 079 3158 4915

RAF Millom Museum, Bankhead Estate
HAVERIGG, MILSOM
4th Sunday of every month (end February-
July), 9am, buyers from 10am
*If wet, the car boot becomes a table top in the
adjacent Prison Officers' Club*
01229 770119

Joss Lane Car Park
SEDBERGH
Wednesdays (year-round), 7.30am
No number listed

Indoor and Outdoor Car Boot
Ulverston Auction, North Lonsdale Rd
ULVERSTON
Sundays (January-December, 50 weeks a year)
6.30am, buyers from 7.30am
077 3856 2304

DENBIGHSHIRE

Doughnut Car Park
CHESTERFIELD
Sundays, 6am
no number listed

Station Yard
DENBIGH
Saturdays
077 866 7378

Gronant Shore Rd
GRONANT
Saturdays (year-round), 7am, buyers from 8am
077 6876 0696

Rhuddlan Community Centre
RHUDDLAN
Sundays, 9am-2pm
079 3093 9061

Rhyl Showfield, Rhuddlan Rd, Opposite
Sainsbury's (A525)
RHYL
Sundays (March-October), 7am
Buyers from 8am
Saturdays (end-May-end-August), 7am
Buyers from 8am
Noble Promotions, 0191 586 8131
www.noble-promotions.homecall.co.uk

DERBYSHIRE

Lady Manners School, Shutts Lane
BAKEWELL
One Sunday a month (April-October), 7.30am
Hard-standing area. No market traders
01629 640253

Farmers' Market Area
BAKEWELL
Sundays (April-December), 7am
No number listed

Indoor Car Boot
Belper Leisure Centre, Kilbourne Rd
BELPER
Last Sunday of the month (January-May;
September-December), 7.30am
070 1422 8967

Springbank Nurseries, Westfield Lane
BALBOROUGH, CHESTERFIELD
Saturdays, 7am
Peak Promotions, 01246 474626

Hollywell Cross Car Park
CHESTERFIELD
Sundays (year-round), 6am
Buyers from 7am
Chesterfield Borough Council, 01246 345999

Outdoor Fleamarket
The Pavements, Beetwell St
CHESTERFIELD
Thursdays, 9am-4pm
01246 345999

Car Park East, The Green
CLOWNE
Thursdays (year-round), 7.30am
Bolsover District Council, 079 7936 5685

Evening Car Boot
Allenton Market Site
DERBY
Tuesdays, 4pm
01332 255519

Cattle Market, The Holmes
W. Meadows Estate (off A52)
DERBY
Sundays (year-round), 7.30am
No vans or trailers
Derby City Council, 01332 255519 / 255574

Indoor Fleamarket
Guildhall
DERBY
Tuesdays
Firthdene, 0113 289 2894

Marsh Lane
ECKINGTON
Sundays, 6am
Peak Promotions, 01246 474626

Truck Stop, Hardwick View Rd
HOLMEWOOD
Sundays, 7am-1pm
Treasure Trove, 01623 629219

Hard-standing Car Boot
Cromford Garden Centre (A6)
CROMFORD, DERBYDALE, MATLOCK
Saturdays (October-December), 7am
Buyers from 8am
Topnotch Management, 079 7276 5940

Moira Miners' Welfare Club, Bath Lane
MOIRA, OVERSEAL
Sundays (May-September), 6am
Buyers from 9am
S&T Promotions, 01283 548024 / 077 8662 8129
www.sandtpromotions.co.uk

Afternoon Car Boot
Twin Oaks Hotel, nr Chesterfield
PALTERTON
Saturdays, 1.30pm, set up from 11.30am
01623 629219

Ripley Hospital, Slack Lane
RIPLEY
One Sunday a month (April-October), 7am
Buyers from 8am
01773 716042

Box Club Car Boot
3, Main St
WOODVILLE, SWADLINCOTE
Sundays (year-round), 7am, buyers from 8am
Indoor table top in winter, outdoor in summer
079 7705 4273

DEVON

Bickleigh Recreation Ground, The Trout Inn
Tiverton to Exeter Rd (A396)
BICKLEIGH, TIVERTON
Saturdays, 8.30am
01884 855357

Indoor Fleamarket
Public Hall
BUDLEIGH SALTERTON
Thursdays, 9am-1pm
01548 561419

Indoor Fleamarket
Jubilee Hall
CHAGFORD
Fridays, 10am-1pm
Hyson Fairs, 01647 231459

Queen Elizabeth's Community College
Lower School
BARNFIELD, CREDITON
Saturdays (May-July), 9.30am
01363 774455

The Sportsmans Arms, Henborough Post
Nr BLACKAWTON, DARTMOUTH
Saturdays (year-round), 7am, buyers from 8am
01803 712231

Evening Car Boot
Warren Rd
DAWLISH WARREN, DAWLISH
Fridays (May-August/September), 4pm-8pm
Devon Fairs, 077 9090 8548

Hard-standing Car Boot & Market
Livestock Centre, Matford Park Rd
MARSH BARTON, EXETER

Sundays (year-round), 6.30am-1pm
Exeter City Council, 01392 665480

Marsh Barton Hard-standing Car Boot
Matford Park, Matford Park Rd, Exeter
Wednesdays (April-October), 8am
Buyers from 9am
Devon Fairs, 077 9090 8548

Westpoint Car Boot
Westpoint, Next to Cat & Fiddle
EXETER
Sundays and Easter Monday, 11am
Buyers from 1pm
If it's raining, the car boot will be in Crealy
078 0217 6993

Nutwell Lodge Car Boot
Exmouth-Exeter Rd (A376)
LYMPSTONE, EXMOUTH
Thursdays (April-June/July), 7am
Buyers from 10am
Devon Fairs, 077 9090 8548

Sandy Car Boot
Littledown Lane
Next to Haven Holiday Camp
LITTLEHAM, EXMOUTH
Saturdays (May-September/October), 7am
Buyers from 10am
Devon Fairs, 077 9090 8548

Afternoon, Under-cover Car Boot
Cattle Market
HATHERLEIGH
Sundays (year-round), 1pm-4pm
079 0011 5529

Cattle Market Car Park
NEWTON ABBOT
Most Sundays (year-round), 6am
Held in the multi-storey car park when raining
Tenbridge District Council, 01626 215427

Newton Abbot Racecourse, Newton Rd-Pottery
Rd Junction
KINGSTEINGTON, NEWTON ABBOT
Sundays (year-round)
No number listed

Plymouth Argyle Car Boot
Central Park
PLYMOUTH
Sundays (year-round), 7am

Buyers to park in the Park & Ride car park
No number listed

Stonehouse Creek Car Boot
Stonehouse Community Centre
STONEHOUSE, PLYMOUTH
Saturdays, Sundays and Bank Holiday
Mondays (year-round), 7am
No food traders, no market traders
01752 606722

Afternoon Car Boot
Pannier Market
TIVERTON
Sundays (April-December), set up from 1pm
Buyers 2pm-3.30pm
01884 258968

Indoor Fleamarket
Pannier Market
TIVERTON
Mondays (not Bank Holidays), 8am-3pm
01884 256666

Indoor Fleamarket
Town Hall, Castle Circus
TORQUAY
Thursdays, 9am-1pm
01548 561419

Indoor Fleamarket
Civic Hall, High St
TOTNES
Fridays, 8.30am-2pm
01803 526214

DORSET

Homeland Farm, Horton Rd, Three Legged
Cross, nr Ringwood
ASHLEY HEATH
Sundays (March-December), 7am
01202 826950

Spetisbury Car Boot
Bournemouth Rd (A350)
SPETISBURY, BLANDFORD
2nd and 4th Sundays in the month (April-
October), 10am
No number listed

Bishop of Winchester Camp, Formerly
Summerbee School, Mallard Rd
BOURNEMOUTH

Saturdays, 7.30am
01202 524855

Linwood School, Alma Rd
WINTON, BOURNEMOUTH
Saturdays, 8.30am
01202 309065

Magna Rd
BOURNEMOUTH
Sundays and May Bank Holiday, 11am
Buyers from 12.30pm
Dogs to be kept on a lead, no food traders
01935 850602

Kinson Primary School, School Lane
KINSON, BOURNEMOUTH
2nd or 3rd Saturday every month, 10.30am
Buyers from 12pm
Kinson School, 01202 771323

West Bay Rd
WEST BAY, BRIDPORT
Sundays (March-December), 8am
Grass and Hard-standing areas available
West Dorset District Council, no number listed

Holmsley Car Boot
Off Christchurch-Lyndhurst Rd (A35)
HOLMSLEY, CHRISTCHURCH
Sundays, 01935 850602

Parley Car Boot
Opposite Bournemouth Airport
WEST PARLEY, CHRISTCHURCH
Sundays, 6.30am
078 5419 0951

Market Site, Weymouth Avenue
DORCHESTER
Sundays (year-round), 7.30am-1pm
No market traders
Ensors, 078 9036 8820 / 01202 841212

Rousdon Car Boot
Curlew Farm, Trinity Hill Rd
ROUSDON, LYME REGIS
Sundays (April-October), 7am
No number listed

Cross Keys, Holt Rd
MANNINGTON
Saturdays, 9am
01202 822555

Hard-standing Car Boot

Greyhound Stadium, Wimbourne Rd
POOLE
Sundays (year-round), 7am-1pm
01202 677449

Afternoon Car Boot
Okadale Middle School, Wimbourne Rd
OAKDALE, POOLE
Saturdays, 1pm, buyers from 2pm
No number listed

St Johns Church, Ashley Rd
PARKSTONE, POOLE
1st Saturdays of the month, 12pm
*Advance booking is necessary. If raining, there will
be a table top in the church hall instead of the
outdoor car boot*
01202 710793

Matchams Hard-standing Car Boot
Matchams Park Raceway
RINGWOOD
Wednesdays, 6am
No number listed

St Leonards Car Boot
Bishops Farm, Between Ringwood and
Ferndown (A31)
ST LEONARDS, RINGWOOD
Saturdays (late-May-late-September), 6.30am
077 3141 8468 / www.stleonardscarboot.co.uk

Car Boot & Market
Beachside Leisure Centre, Bowleaze Covey
PRESTON, WEYMOUTH
Mondays (Easter-October), 7am

Beachside Leisure Centre, 01305 833216
Bagwell Farm (B3157)
CHICKERELL, WEYMOUTH
Sundays (May-August), 11am
Buyers from 12pm
Saturdays, 8am, buyers from 9am
078 1691 0174

Car Boot & Market
Wimborne Market, Riverside Park
WIMBORNE
Fridays and Sundays, 7.30am-4pm
Ensors, 01202 841212

DUMFRIES & GALLOWAY

*To be a regular seller at car boots in this
county (and the whole of Scotland), you
need to register with Trading Standards
(see p113 for more details)*

Dumfries Park Farm Showground
New Abbey Rd
DUMFRIES
2 or 3 Sundays every month (April-October),
8.15am
077 5237 4794 / www.giantcarboots.com

EAST LOTHIAN

See Midlothian

*To be a regular seller at car boots in this
county (and the whole of Scotland), you
need to register with Trading Standards
(see p113 for more details)*

ESSEX

Ardleigh Showground, Old Ipswich Rd
ARDLEIGH, nr COLCHESTER
Sundays, 6am-1pm
Boot Group, 077 4863 7856 / 01206 864993
www.bootgroup.com

Vicarage Field Shopping Centre, Ripple Rd
Lower Car Park
BARKING
Sundays, 7.30am
077 0930 1603

Forest Farm, Forest Rd
BARKINGSIDE
Tuesdays, 7am-2pm
020 8501 4090

Stevenson's Farm, Arterial Rd/Nevendon Rd
by Nevendon Flyover (A127/A132)
BASILDON
Sundays, Thursdays and Bank Holiday
Mondays and Good Friday, 7am
No food or pet food traders
01268 285145 / www.nevendonbootsale.com

See also Dunton

Afternoon Car Boot
Barleylands Showground (A129)
BILLERICAY
Sundays and Bank Holiday Mondays (March-October), 10am, buyers from 10.30am
Wednesdays (from May), 10am
077 6382 7431
www.barleylands.co.uk/boot_sale.asp

Blake House Craft Centre (Off Old A120)
BLAKE END, BRAINTREE
Saturdays and Bank Holiday Mondays
(March-September), 11am
077 5723 2050

Baytree Farm, Coggeshall Rd (A120)
BRAINTREE
Saturdays (April-November), 6am
No number listed

Chequers Field Car Boot
Chequers Inn, Chequers Rd
SOUTH WEALD, BRAINTREE
Saturdays (March-summer), 7am
079 5426 4506

Chequers Rd, Past the Bear Pub
NOAK HILL, BRENTWOOD
Sundays (March-May), 6am
077 5883 2840

Orsett Cock Roundabout
Brentwood Rd (A128)
ORSETT, BRENTWOOD
Sundays, 8am
078 1237 6411

Peartree Car Boot
Brentwood Rd (A128)
BULPHAN
Saturdays, 6am
077 6512 1179 / 077 6612 1430
www.peartreebootsale.co.uk

Sadlers Farm (A127)
CANVEY ISLAND
Saturdays (year-round), 7am
No number listed

Boreham
CHELMSFORD
Sundays
No number listed

Wheelers Farm, Wheelers Farm Hill East

(Off A130)
LITTLE WALTHAM, CHELMSFORD
Sundays (starts April) and Bank Holiday
Mondays, 6am, buyers from 7am
078 1757 7111 / 7079

Bric-a-brac Market
Market Site
CHELMSFORD
Thursdays, 8am
01245 256558

Chigwell Rise, Next to the
David Lloyd Health Club
CHIGWELL
Saturdays, (End March-August), 7am
Country Group, 020 8521 8947 / 01279 871117

Hard-standing Car Boot
Netherstone Farm, Sewardstone Rd
CHINGFORD
Sundays (March-September), 8.30am
Buyers from 10am
Netherstone Farm, 075 1230 1418

Birch Park, Maldon Rd (B1022)
BIRCH, COLCHESTER
Sundays (May-September), 6.30am
Wylde Productions, 077 6844 8221
www.essexcarbootsale.com

Marks Tey, London Rd
COLCHESTER
Wednesdays (year-round), 7am
01206 864993 / www.bootgroup.com

London Rd (Old A13), Just Off 5 Bells
Interchange (A13)
CORRINGHAM
Wednesdays (Easter-October), 6am
Recently relocated after 19 years, about a mile from the original site
01702 616301

Dunton Rd, nr Basildon (off A127)
DUNTON
Sundays and Bank Holiday Mondays, 6am
01277 624979

Afternoon, Hard-standing Car Boot
Barrow Rd Staff Car Park
Pinnacles Industrial Estate
HARLOW
Sundays (year-round apart from
Christmas-time), 10.30am

Buyers from 12pm
Countryside, Promotions, 01992 468619
www.countrysidepromotions.co.uk

Just Off A12, Junction 23, Northbound Exit
KELVEDON
Tuesdays (April-October), 12pm
25% discount for advance bookings
01376 570334 / www.kelvedonrotary.com

Afternoon Car Boot
Canes Field
NORTH WEALD
Sundays, 12pm-5pm
Countryside, Promotions, 01992 468619
www.countrysidepromotions.co.uk

Bluemans Field, Talbot Roundabout (A414)
NORTH WEALD
Saturdays (from May), 10.30am
Buyers from 12pm
Countryside, Promotions, 01992 468619
www.countrysidepromotions.co.uk

Hard-standing Car Boot
North Weald Airfield
NORTH WEALD
Saturdays, 6am-4pm
Hughmark, 0118 945 1799

Market Site
PITSEA
Fridays and Sundays, 8am-2pm
Charfleet, 01268 773363 or 552146

The Bell Inn, Broadway
RAINHAM
Thursdays (year-round), 5am
Buyers from 6.30am
30 pitches, book in advance
01708 525496

Willow Farm Car Boot
Mardyke Farm, Ship Lane, Opposite Thurrock
Hotel nr Dartford Tunnel
WENNINGTON, RAINHAM
Sundays (from February)
Country Club Group, 077 8054 6284

The Carpenters Arms, London Rd
RAYLEIGH
Sundays (April-September), 9.30am
Gables Cars, 01268 786679

Late Morning Car Boot
Whitehouse Farm (Old A130)

RETTENDON
Saturdays and Sundays
(mid-March-October), 10.30am
Lazybones, 079 5682 6730

Ardleigh Green Car Boot
Ardleigh House, 42, Ardleigh Green Rd
HORNCHURCH, ROMFORD
Saturdays, 8am
Tables supplied if needed
079 3127 0181

Decathlon Indoor Car Boot
Decathlon Centre
Angel Way/St Edwards Way, Nr Brewery
ROMFORD
Saturdays, Sundays, Wednesdays
and Fridays, 7am
Free parking for traders, up to 200 stalls
079 4114 92538 / 079 3287 6058

Brier Estate Car Boot
Mertle Rd, Harold Hill
ROMFORD
Fridays (year-round), 8am
Buyers from 9am
No number listed

Bonzer Car Boot
Whalebone Lane North, Collier Row
ROMFORD
Sundays (June-October), 7am
077 5883 2840

Eastern Avenue West
ROMFORD
Thursdays, 6am-2pm
020 8501 4090

Sadlers Farm Roundabout (A13/A130)
SOUTH BENFLEET
Saturdays (from April), 6am
Country Group, 077 8054 6284

Village Hall, South Hanningfield Rd
SOUTH HANNINGFIELD
Sundays, 7am
01268 710995

Southend United Football Club,
Victoria Avenue
SOUTHEND-ON-SEA
Saturdays
No number listed

Upshires Rd Sites, Upshire Rd

UPSHIRE, WALTHAM ABBEY
Sundays, 10.30am, buyers from 12pm
Countryside Promotions, 01992 468619
www.countrysidepromotions.co.uk

Kirby Rd
WALTON ON THE NAZE
Fridays (April-September), 7am
078 3316 1656

Wanstead Rugby Club, Roding Lane North
Off Woodford Ave
BUCKHURST HILL, WANSTEAD
Saturdays, 7am
Country Group, 01279 871117

Hawk Farm, Hawks Lane
WEELEY
Saturdays (year-round), 6am-1pm
Boot Group, 077 4863 7856 / 01206 864993
www.bootgroup.com

FIFE

To be a regular seller at car boots in this county (and the whole of Scotland), you need to register with Trading Standards (see p113 for more details)

Trash and Treasure Car Boot
Newbridge Inn Car Park
GLANWOOD, GLENROTHES
Saturdays and Sundays (year-round), 8.30am
No number listed

Beleknowes Park & Ride Car Park
Admiralty Rd (A921)
INVERKEITHING
Sundays, 8am, buyers from 9am
No number listed

Lochgelly Public Park
LOCHGELLY
Sundays, 8am
No number listed

Tayport Football Ground, The Canniepart,
Shanwell Rd
TAYPORT
Every 2nd Sunday of the month (March-September), 8am, buyers from 10am
No food or market traders. No dogs allowed
01382 553670 / 079 5138 0193

GLAMORGANSHIRE

Cwm Car Boot
Cwmaman Institute, Alice Place
CWMAMAN, ABERDARE
Sundays (from late-April-December), 9am
Buyers from 10am
Inside stalls available during bad weather
Cwmaman Institute, 01685 876003 / 887100

Fontgary Caravan Site, Fonmon
RHOOSE, BARRY
1st and 3rd Sundays of the month
(April-September), 7am
No number listed

Glenbrook Inn, Dobbins Rd
BARRY
Saturdays (from February), 8am
Buyers from 9am
01446 747808

Pyle, Stormy Down
BRIDGEND
Sundays, 7am-2pm
S & W, 01656 746028

Under-cover Car Boot
Multi-storey Car Park, Cheapside
BRIDGEND
Sundays (Year-round apart from Christmas Eve
and New Year's Eve), 7am-2pm
*No traders, new goods or food. Sellers arrive
between 7am-10am but may not leave before noon*
Bridgend Festivals Committee, 01656 661338
www.bridgend-events.co.uk

Mountain Ash Car Boot
Our Lady of Lourdes, Miskin Rd
MOUNTAIN ASH, CARDIFF
2nd Saturdays of the month, 8am
Buyers from 9am
Parking for buyers within walking distance
No number listed

Hard-standing Car Boot
Vegetable Market, Bessemer Rd
CARDIFF
Saturdays (year-round), 9.30am
Sundays (year-round), 8am
Some under-cover stalls available if wet
079 6712 3016

Ocean Way, Splott
CARDIFF
Saturdays, from 8am
02920 777123

Splott Car Boot
Lewis Rd
SPLOTT, CARDIFF
Thursdays and Saturdays (year-round), 6am
Buyers from 7am
No number listed

St Mellons Car Boot
Strathy Rd Car Park, Strathy Rd
ST MELLONS, CARDIFF
Wednesdays (Spring-winter), 8am
Buyers from 9am
No number listed

Co-ed Glass School, Ty Glas Avenue
LLANISHEN, CARDIFF
2nd Saturdays of the month
(March-December), 8am
02920 758706

Indoor Car Boot and Market
Rheola Works, A465
RESOLVEN
Saturdays, 7am-2pm
Wendy Fair, 01895 632221

Sully Plastics, South Rd
SULLY
Sundays (April/May-September), 7am
Buyers from 8am
No number listed

Indoor and Outdoor Car Boot
Clydach (Junc 45, M4)
SWANSEA
Wednesdays, 6am
079 7924 3265

Car Boot & Market
Clydach (Junc 45, M4)
SWANSEA
Sundays, 7.30am
Town & Country, 079 7148 5181

New Lodge Social Club (Old Legion)
Alexandra Rd
GORSEINON, SWANSEA
Saturdays, 8am
078 9680 9794

Hard-standing Car Boot
Singleton Hospital, Sketty Lane
SWANSEA
Saturdays (year-round), 6am
Buyers from 7am-2pm
01792 205666

Hard-standing Car Boot
Superstore, Garngoch
GORSEINON, SWANSEA
Sundays, 7am-1pm
Julians, 01792 894927

GLASGOW

See Lanarkshire

To be a regular seller at car boots in this city (and the whole of Scotland), you need to register with Trading Standards (see p113 for more details)

GLOUCESTERSHIRE

Afternoon Car Boot
Former MOD Site, nr Chalford (off A419)
ASTON DOWN
Sundays, 12.30pm-4.30pm
077 1147 6715

Car Boot & Market
Cheltenham Racecourse, Prestbury Park
CHELTENHAM
Sundays (year-round), 6am
Buyers from 7am
079 6614 5286

Southam, Southam Lane Nr Racecourse
CHELTENHAM
Saturdays (week before Easter-October)
9am-1pm
Sundays (week before Easter-October), 12pm
Stanton Fairs, 01766 523409
www.bootsrus.co.uk

The Beeches Football Club, Stratton Meadows
Grove Lane
STRATTON, CIRENCESTER
Every other Sunday (May-September), 8am
Buyers from 9am
01285 652494

Old Cattle Market, Ladybelle St Car Park
BLACKFRIARS, GLOUCESTER
Wednesdays and Sundays, 6am
No number listed

Hard-standing Car Boot
Oldends Lane Car Park
STONEHOUSE
Saturdays, set up 8am
077 1147 6715

Table Top Car Boot
Scout Hut, Oldbury Rd
TEWKSBURY
Wednesdays and Saturdays (year-round)
8.30am, buyers from 9.30am
Same day as the nearby market
01684 294318

The Big Field (B4058)
WOTTON-UNDER-EDGE
Sundays, 8.30am
077 1147 6715

GREATER MANCHESTER

To be a regular seller at car boots in this county, you need to register with Trading Standards (see p113 for more details)

Fleamarket
Old Market Place
ALTRINCHAM
Thursdays
0161 941 4261

Secondhand Market
Grey Mare Lane
BESWICK
Fridays
0161 223 5742

Hard-standing Car Boot
Lever St
GREAT LEVER, BOLTON
Sundays (year-round), 5.30am
Buyers from 7.30am
No number listed

Gorton Cross St
GORTON
Mondays
0161 231 3522

Outdoor Fleamarket
Church Lane
HARPURMEY
Thursdays
Manchester Markets, 0161 205 0215

Outdoor Fleamarket
Dickenson Rd
LONGSIGHT
Tuesdays
Manchester Markets, 0161 225 9859

Atherton Motor Auctions, Coal Pit Lane
Off Wigan Rd
ATHERTON
Sundays (year-round), 6am, buyers from 7am
070 5020 8905 / 01942 894455
www.athertoncarbootsale.co.uk

Bric-a-brac Car Boot
George H. Carnall Leisure Centre
Kings Way Park
DAVYHULME, MANCHESTER
Saturdays (March-December), 7am
Buyers from 8am
0161 749 2555

Bowlee Car Boot & Collectors Market
Bowlee Community Park Showground
Heywood Old Rd (A6405)
MIDDLETON, MANCHESTER
Sundays (May-August), 7am
No new goods. Note, not open all Sundays in July.
Actively looking for new catering concessions at the
time of writing, ring for details
01253 782828
www.hoylespromotions.co.uk/bowlee-carboot.html

Gorse Hill Primary School, Burleigh Rd
STREFORD, MANCHESTER
Sundays (year-round), 6am
Buyers from 6.30am
077 3342 1598

Car Boot & Market
New Smithfield Market, Whitworth St
OPENSHAW, MANCHESTER
Sundays, 6am, buyers from 7am
Manchester Markets, 0161 234 7357

Buile Hill Park, Eccles Rd
SALFORD
Sundays (April-August), 7.30am

Buyers from 8.30am
Must be booked in advance.
No traders or electrical goods.
Friends of Buile Hill Park, 079 6832 7107
(before 8pm)

Fleamarket
Market Site
SALFORD
Thursdays
0161 736 7845

Holly Lane
STYAL, MANCHESTER
Sundays (May-September), 6am
0161 724 6169

Civic Centre, Pondswick Lane
WYTHENSHAWE
Mondays
0161 499 2832

GWENT

Indoor Fleamarket
Market Hall, Cross St
ABERGAVENNY
Wednesdays, 8am-4pm
01873 735811

Govilon, Aber-Brynmawr Rd (A465)
ABERGAVENNY
Thursdays, 9am
01873 830834

Crown Roundabout (Nr A472/A4049)
PONTLLANFRAITH, BLACKWOOD
Sundays (July-October), 7am, buyers from 8am
No buyers' parking on site
No number listed

Fairwater High School, Ty-Gwyn Way
FAIRWATER, CWMBRAN
Sundays, 6.30am
Use the toilets in the nearby leisure centre
No number listed

Newport Cattle Market
NEWPORT
Sundays, 6am
No number listed

Under-cover Car Boot
Newport Car Auctions, Usk Way

NEWPORT
Sundays (year-round), 6am, buyers from 9am
No number listed

Afternoon Car Boot
Talywain Golf Club, Albert Rd
TALYWAIN, PONTYPOOL
Every other Saturday, 1pm, buyers from 2pm
No number listed

Afternoon Car Boot
Station Rd
RAGLAN
Sundays, 1.30pm, buyers from 2pm
No number listed

Barbarian House, Llantarnum Rd
CWBRAN, TORFAEN
Sundays (February-December), 7.30am
No number listed

GWYNEDD

Criccieth Memorial Hall
CRICCIETH
Sundays
078 1337 8684

Porthmadog Football Club
POrTHMADOG
Sundays and Bank Holiday Mondays
01766 512991

HAMPSHIRE

Aldershot Town Football Club
ALDERSHOT
Sundays, 7.30am
077 1094 7571

Under-cover Car Boot
Multi-storey Car Park, High St
ALDERSHOT
Sundays (year-round), 11am
The car boot is on the bottom level of the car park, opposite the main shopping centre, buyers' parking on the upper levels
079 6650 6808

Hillside Nurseries
ALTON
Sundays and Bank Holiday Mondays, 7am
Buyers from 8am-1pm

Tuesdays, 9am, buyers from 10am
01420 82011

Wyke Down Caravan Park (Off A303)
PICKET PIECE, ANDOVER
Sundays and Bank Holiday Mondays, 9.30am
No number listed

Afternoon Car Boot
Museum of Army Flying (A343)
MIDDLE WALLOP, NR ANDOVER
Approx. 3rd Wednesday of the month, 2.30pm
01264 784421

Afternoon Car Boot
Popley Community Centre, Popley Fields
BASINGSTOKE
Sundays and Bank Holiday Mondays, 12.30pm
Inside stalls available during wet weather
Popley Community Car Boot, 01256 414494

Strawberry Fields, Brockenhurst-Lymington Rd
(A337)
BOLDRE
Sundays (Easter-November), 7am
023 8081 3655

Country Markets (A325)
KINGSLEY, BORDON
Sundays and Bank Holiday Mondays (year-round), 8am
Wednesdays (year-round), 10am
01420 472486 / www.countrymarket.co.uk

Car Boot & Market
Junc 8, M27, nr Southampton
BURLESDON
Sundays, 7am-2pm
01489 786653

Brookfield Car Boot
Brookfield, Allington Lane
FAIR OAK, EASTLEIGH
Sundays
No dogs allowed
023 8060 1159

Afternoon Car Boot
Pinehurst, Roundabout Nr Airport, Opposite
King's Mead Shopping Centre
FARNBOROUGH
Sundays (year-round apart from Christmas and
New Year), 10am, buyers from 11am-4pm
No new goods
079 7924 3270

Afternoon Car Boot
Wavell School, Lynchford Rd
FARNBOROUGH
Saturdays, 11am, buyers from 12pm
*Height restriction of 6'6" as the car boot is held on
the school's netball courts*
No number listed

Calthorpe Park School
Hitches Lane
FLEET
1st Sunday of the month
No number listed

Victoria Rd Car Park, Victoria Rd
FLEET
Sundays (April-October)
WSM Fairs, 01252 373529

Afternoon Car Boot
Next to the Sports Ground
FORDINGBRIDGE
Sundays (September-December), 11am
Buyers from 12pm
Southcoast Events, 079 1762 5325

Bridgemary Community School/Sports
College, Wych Lane
GOSPORT
Sundays (year-round), 7.30am-1pm
Hard-standing available in winter
Bridgemary Community School, 078 8178 6556

Beachlands, Seafront
HAYLING ISLAND
Wednesdays, 8am-2pm
No number listed

Multiple Sclerosis Charity Car Boot
Gangwarily Community Centre
HOLBURY
Sundays, 9am
No number listed

Hook Junior School, Church View
HOOK
1st Sunday of the month (May-August)
HSPA, 01256 762468

Merchistoun Hall, Portsmouth Rd
HORDEAN
Fridays, 8am-12pm
02392 597114

Indoor and Outdoor Car Boot
Hillside Youth Club, Cheltenham Rd
PAULSGROVE, PORTSMOUTH
Saturdays, 8am, buyers from 10am
078 5760 5257

Shootash Car Boot
Shootash Crossroads, Salisbury Rd (A27)
ROMSEY
Saturdays (April-November), 8am-3pm
077 7472 9598

Car Boot & Market
Bursledon Open Air Market, Hamble Lane
BURSLEDON, SOUTHAMPTON
Sundays (year-round), 7am
No dogs allowed
01489 786653

Ringwood Rd, Opposite Netley Marsh
Steam Engine
SOUTHAMPTON
Sundays, 7am, buyers from 8.30am
No number listed

The Saint Table Top Car Boot
The Saint, Kendal Ave
SOUTHAMPTON
Sundays (year-round), 10.30am
Buyers from 12pm
Ring for booking information
078 6135 4417

Lawns Car Boot
Forest Rd
DENMEAD, WATERLOOVILLE
Sundays (June-October), 7am
079 7050 6601 / 077 9161 4978

Indoor Bric-a-brac Market
Community Centre, Mill Lane
WICKHAM
Saturdays, 11am-4.30pm
Athena Fairs, 01489 584633

Bullington Cross Inn (A303/A34)
SUTTON SCOTNEY, WINCHESTER
1st and 3rd Sundays of the month, 6am
Buyers from 7am
Thursdays, 9am-1pm
01962 760285

St Swithun's Church Car Park
Hall Lane/Firgrove Rd
YATELEY

1st Saturday of the month
01252 872732

HEREFORDSHIRE

See Also Worcestershire

To be a regular seller at car boots in the city of Hereford, you need to register with Trading Standards (see p113 for more details)

Auction Site (A49)
LEOMINSTER
Sundays, 7.30am-12pm
01568 611325

Hard-standing Car Boot
The Grandstand Pub, Grandstand Rd
HEREFORD
Saturdays (June-September), 9am
Buyers from 10am
01432 370867

Hard-standing Car Boot
Cattle Market, Edgar St
HEREFORD
Sundays, 8am, buyers from 9am
079 6804 4697

Auction Site (A49)
LEOMINSTER
Sundays, 7.30am-12pm
01568 611325

Afternoon Car Boot
Stoney St, Nr Hereford
MADLEY
Sundays, 12.30pm, buyers from 2pm
No early buyers
01432 357088 / 078 8424 5715

Allweather Car Boot
Livestock Centre (A40)
ROSS ON WYE
Sundays (year-round), 9.30am
Big Bens, 01981 250591

The Buttley Tearoom (A438)
WINFORTON
Sundays (late-May-September), 10am
Buyers from 11am
01544 327879

HERTFORDSHIRE

U-Boot
Buntingford Rd (A507)
BALDOCK
Saturdays (Easter-October), 6am
Buyers from 7am
No foam-filled furniture
01462 790260 / www.u-boot.co.uk

Station Car Parks
BISHOPS STORTFORD
Sundays (year-round except Christmas and
New Year), 7am-2pm
Countryside Promotions, 01992 468619
www.countrysidepromotions.co.uk

Indoor Fleamarket
Village Hall, Shenley Road
BOREHAMWOOD
Wednesdays, 7.30am-3.30pm
020 8386 3686

Oakmead Lodge (A507)
COTTERED, BUNTINGFORD
Sundays (from May), 9am, buyers from 10am
079 5273 5672

Indoor Car Boot
Grundy Park Leisure Centre
CHESHUNT
Sundays, 9.30am
Countryside Promotions, 01992 468619

Hill View Farm, Northaw Rd
WEST NORTHAW, CUFFLEY
Sundays and Bank Holiday Mondays
(April-October), 7am-1pm
Jumbo Car Boots, 01707 873360
www.jumbocarbootsales.co.uk

Events Field, Aldenham Rd, Off Watford Rd
ELSTREE VILLAGE
Saturdays (Easter-October), 6am
Buyers from 7am
079 3253 2421 / 020 8578 5720

Graveley Hill Fruit Farm (off B197)
GRAVELEY
Saturdays (March-October), 9am
Buyers from 10am
S. Enterprises, 01438 318441 / 079 5273 5672

Afternoon Car Boot
Birchwood Sports Centre
HATFIELD
Sundays (April-October), 11.30am-4pm
Countryside Promotions, 01992 468619
www.countrysidepromotions.co.uk

Lower Rd, Nash Mills
HEMEL HEMPSTEAD
Sundays (April-October), 6am
01923 265707 / 079 6350 1858

Marchmont Car Boot
Link Rd
HEMEL HEMPSTEAD
Sundays (May-September), 6.30am
Buyers from 7.30am
No number listed

Market Square, Marlowes
HEMEL HEMPSTEAD
Sundays, 9am-1pm
Town & Country, 079 8073 1353

Fleamarket
Market Square, Marlowes
HEMEL HEMPSTEAD
Wednesdays, 9am-2pm
01952 242019

Hitchin Town Football Club, Fishponds Rd
HITCHIN
Wednesdays (from May), 5pm
079 5273 5672

Millstream Car Boot
Millstream Car Park, Cambridge Rd
HITCHIN
Bank Holiday Mondays, 9.30am
Buyers from 10.30am
075 0405 3113

Car Boot & Market
Market Place
HITCHIN
Sundays (year-round), 8am
Buyers from 10am-3pm
078 7947 6757

Outdoor Fleamarket
Market Place
HITCHIN
Fridays (year-round)
Firthdene, 0113 289 2894

Afternoon Car Boot
Elm Court, 363, Mutton Lane
POTTERS BAR
Every other Saturday (April-October), 12pm
Buyers from 1.30pm
Elm Court, 01707 659602
www.elmcourt.org.uk

Afternoon Car Boot
Swanley Bar Lane, Off Gt North Rd (A1000)
SWANLEY BAR, POTTERS BAR
Sundays, 11am, buyers from 12pm
020 8372 0323

Hertfordshire Showground, Off Junction 9, M1
REDBOURN
Sundays (May-October), 6am, buyers from 8am
01582 612687

Hard-standing Car Boot
Station Car Park
RICKMANSWORTH
Sundays, 7am-12.30pm
No number listed

St Albans City Hospital, Waverley Rd
ST ALBANS
1st Sunday of the month, 8.30am
No number listed

Afternoon Hard-standing Car Boot
Former Kodak Site, Bessemer Drove, Off
Gunnelswood Rd
STEVENAGE
Sundays (year-round except for Christmas and
New Year), 10.30am, buyers from 12pm-4pm
Countryside Promotions, 01992 468619
www.countrysidepromotions.co.uk

Hard-standing Car Boot
Stevenage Borough Football Club
Broadhall Way
STEVENAGE
Saturdays, Sundays and Bank Holiday
Mondays (year-round), 8am, buyers from 9am
Lennox Pomotions Ltd, 079 4617 0785
www.lennoxpromotionslimited.com

Fleamarket
Town Centre, Nr Station
STEVENAGE
Wednesdays and Saturdays, 9am-2pm
No number listed

North Side Car Parks, Stanborough Rd
STANBOROUGH, WELWYN GARDEN CITY
Sundays, 11.30am, buyers from 12pm
Sellers cannot enter the selling area before 11.30am
Countryside Promotions, 01992 468619
www.countrysidepromotions.co.uk

INVERNESS-SHIRE

*To be a regular seller at car boots in this
county (and the whole of Scotland), you
need to register with Trading Standards
(see p113 for more details)*

Highland Council Car Park, Glenurquhart Rd
INVERNESS
Sundays (March-December), 9am
079 6601 1779

ISLE OF WIGHT

Main Car Park, High St, Next to the Church
BRADING
Saturdays (year-round), 7am, buyers from 8am
CBS, 078 8772 5924

Newport Football Club, St George's Park
NEWPORT
Sundays (year-round), 6am, buyers from 7am
Tuesdays (June-September), 6am
Buyers from 7am
CBS, 078 8772 5924

Seafront, Next to LA Bowl
RYDE
Sundays (March-December), 11.45am
Thursdays (June-October), 6pm
01983 868850

KENT

*To be a regular seller at car boots in this
county, you need to register with Trading
Standards (see p113 for more details)*

Tara Car Boot
Crest Farm, London Rd
ADDINGTON
Saturdays (July-September), 6.30am
01622 812277

Ashford Football Club, The Homelands
Kingsnorth
ASHFORD
Sundays, 6.30am
078 1863 7442

Hard-standing Market and Car Boot
Orbital Park (Junc 10, M20)
ASHFORD
Saturdays and Sundays, 7am-2pm
01233 506219

Indoor Car Boot
Azelia Hall, 258, Croydon Rd, Elmers End
BECKENHAM
Sundays (September-April), 11am
Buyers from 12pm
Advance booking essential
020 8658 7647

Hayes St Farm, Hayes Lane (Off B265)
BROMLEY
Every other Sunday, also Bank Holiday
Mondays (April-September), 7am
020 8462 1186

By Perry St Roundabout, Wyatt Rd
CRAYFORD
Saturdays
LDL Promotions, 01322 406682

Barville Farm, Timnastone (A256)
DOVER
Sundays, 6am
MB County, 01304 829822

Former St Mary's Westbrook Field
Shorncliffe Rd
FOLKESTONE
Saturdays (May-July), 7am
Westbrook House Parents' Society, 079 1426
9015 / www.westbrookparents.org

Westmoor Farm, Moor St (A2)
GILLINGHAM
Sundays (March-October), 6am
No food or drink traders
01634 378886

Laysdown Rd
LAYSDOWN
Sundays
01795 511060

Powdermill Lane
LEIGH
Saturdays
01732 833855

Axton Chase Fields, Main Rd
LONGFIELD
Saturdays, set up 11am, official start time 1pm
020 8309 5696

Sutton Rd (A274)
MAIDSTONE
Sundays
077 6955 1957

Hewitts Farm, Court Rd
ORPINGTON
Sundays
01959 532003

Tripes Farm, Chelsfield Lane
ORPINGTON
Sundays (March-October), 6am
01689 876602
www.tripesfarm.co.uk/bootsale.html

Indoor Market
Orpington Halls, High St
ORPINGTON
Saturdays, 7am-3pm
SRP Fairs, 01689 854924

Amhuerst Auctions, Featherstone House
375, High St
ROCHESTER
Sundays, 1pm
Amhuerst Auctions, 01634 815713

Kent Stately Home Car Boot
Hole Park (B2086)
BENENDEN, Nr ROLVENDEN
*Bi-annual charity car boot at a Kent stately home
(not always Hole Park)*
www.kentstatelyhomecarbootsale.co.uk

Thrift Farm, Straight Lane (A259)
BROOKLAND, ROMNEY MARSH
Saturdays, Sundays and Bank Holiday
Mondays (April-October), 7am
Buyers from 8.30am
Thrift Farm, 01797 344276

Flamingo Park (A20)
SIDCUP

Sundays (April-August), 10.30am
No food or drink traders. No dogs allowed
020 8309 1012

Staplehurst Station Car Park
STAPLEHURST
Sundays, 7am
01474 709938 / 01622 831674

Precinct Car Park
STROOD
Sundays, 8am-4pm
01709 700072

Birchwood Arena, Birchwood Rd
SWANLEY
Sundays, 7am, buyers from 8am
*No food or drink traders. Dogs must be kept
on a lead*
079 4092 5464

Pedham Place Farm, London Rd (A20)
SWANLEY
Sundays, 7am
No food or drink traders
SMB Boot Fairs, 01795 426400
www.bootfairs.net/smb

TCC School, Yarnton Way
THAMESMEAD
Sundays
020 8855 1552

King Ethelberts School, Canterbury Rd
BIRCHINGTON, THANET
3rd Sunday of the month (September-July),
7am
No food or drink traders. No electrical goods
01843 831999

Indoor Fleamarket
The Angel Centre
TONBRIDGE
Fridays (not Good Friday), 8am-1pm
01732 456196

Longfield Rd
TUNBRIDGE WELLS
Every other Sunday (April-September), 6am
Buyers from 7am
No number listed

Greenways Car Boot
London Rd

WEST MALLING
Sundays
01622 812277

Meadow Crest Farm, London Rd
ADDINGTON, WEST MALLING
Saturdays (April-July), 6.30am
Buyers from 7.30am
077 9596 7609

Wrotham Hill (A20)
WROTHAM
Sundays, 7am, buyers from 8am
No food or drink traders
SMB Boot Fairs, 01795 426400
www.bootfairs.net/smb

KINROSS

*To be a regular seller at car boots in this
county (and the whole of Scotland), you
need to register with Trading Standards
(see p113 for more details)*

Bridgend
KINROSS
Saturdays
01577 866557

Under-cover Car Boot
Kinross Market (Off B996)
KINROSS
Saturdays, 6am, buyers from 8am
No new goods
No number listed

LANARKSHIRE

*To be a regular seller at car boots in this
county (and the whole of Scotland), you
need to register with Trading Standards.
You will need separate registration for
selling at car boots and markets in
Glasgow on a regular basis (see p113 for
more details)*

Under-cover and Outdoor Car Boot
Blochairn Fruit Market, 130 Blochain Rd
BLOCHAIRN, GLASGOW
Sundays, 6am-3pm
Glasgow Markets, 0141 287 2500

www.glasgow.gov.uk/en/Business/Markets/S
undaycarbootsale

Excelsior Stadium, Craigneuk Ave
AIRDRIE, GLASGOW
Sundays, 9am
079 4730 0701

Barras Centre Car Boot
54, Calton Entry, The Barras
GLASGOW
Saturdays (year-round), 8am
Buyers from 9am
The Phone Booth, 0141 548 8787

Lanark Agricultural Centre
Hyndford Rd (A73)
LANARK
Sundays (year-round except for Christmas)
7am, buyers from 8am
*Whilst a year-round car boot, it is weather
dependent, so check it's on before travelling*
Lawrie & Symington, 077 1865 9066

Lanark Rd
CLYDESDALE, OVERTOWN
Sundays and Bank Holiday Mondays (April-
September), 8am
No number listed

Main Rd
WISHAW
Saturdays (January-September), 7am
No number listed

LANCASHIRE

*To be a regular seller at car boots in this
county, you need to register with Trading
Standards (see p113 for more details)*

Car Boot & Fleamarket
Market Place, Peel St
ACCRINGTON
Thursdays and Sundays, 7am-2.30/3pm
01254 233816

Fleamarket
Temple Court
BACUP
Fridays, 9am-3pm
01706 873499

Bilsborrow (A6)
BILSBORROW
Sundays (May-September), 6am
0870 744 2685

Greenhalgh Farm, Fleetwood Rd
GREENHALGH, BLACKPOOL
Saturdays (April-September)
079 3158 4915

Back Lane
GREENHALGH, BLACKPOOL
Sundays (from April), 7am
No number listed

Indoor and Outdoor Car Boot
Winbourne Leisure Park, Cropper Rd
MARTON, BLACKPOOL
Saturdays (September-April), 6.30am
Buyers from 7.30am
*Bookings can be made in advance for this 75-pitch
car boot*
DW Promotions, 079 4685 7010

Formerly Cropper Manor Garden Centre
MARTON, BLACKPOOL
Saturdays (March-November), 7am
*No garden centre-related products can be sold,
including garden furniture, plants and lawn
mowers*
079 3142 7627

Indoor Car Boot
Staining Village Hall, Chain Lane
STAINING, BLACKPOOL
Every other Sunday (September-Easter), 8am
buyers from 8.30am
Booking in advance is recommended
079 8435 5264

Indoor Car Boot
Thornton Sports Centre, Victoria Rd East
THORNTON, BLACKPOOL
Every other Sunday (September-Easter)
7.45am, buyers from 8.30am
Book in advance
079 8435 5264

Grass and Hard-standing Car Boot
World of Water, Preston New Rd (A583)
WESTBY, BLACKPOOL
Sundays (October-Easter), 8am
Next to two caravan parks
079 3142 7627

Whyndyke Farm, Preston New Rd
BLACKPOOL
Sundays (Easter-October), 7am
No new fishing equipment allowed
01253 767279

Ashbourne St, by Bus Station
BOLTON
Sundays
01204 336825

Indoor Car Boot
Upper Floor, Denmark Mill, Cawdor St
FARNWORTH, BOLTON
Sundays (year-round), 7am
Buyers from 9am-1pm
077 4766 2004

Moor Lane, Town Centre
BOLTON
Sundays (year-round), 7am
No number listed

Bric-a-brac Market
Market Square
BURNLEY
Wednesdays, 8am-3pm
01282 664651

Fleamarket
BURY
Wednesdays and Fridays, 9am-3pm
Bury Markets, 0161 253 6520

Carnforth Working Men's Club
CARNFORTH
Sundays, 8am
01524 720686

Queen's Hotel
CARNFORTH
Saturdays
01524 732978

Elaine's Car Boot
Opposite Botany Bay, Blackburn Rd
Junction 8, M61
CHORLEY
Sundays (spring-September), 6am
0161 724 6169

Under-cover Car Boot & Fleamarket
Flat Iron Market, Off Jubilee St
CHORLEY
Mondays except for Bank Holidays (year-

round), 7am, buyers from 8am-4pm
Firthdene, 0113 289 2894

Indoor and Outdoor Hard-standing Car Boot & Collectors Market
Clitheroe Auction Mart, Ribblesdale Court
Lincoln Way
CLITHEROE
Sundays (year-round), 7am
Buyers from 8am-4pm
Hoyles Promotions, 01253 782828
www.hoylespromotions.co.uk/clitheroe.html

Car Boot & Market
Gisburn Cotes (A59)
GISBURN, CLITHEROE
Sundays (April-August/September), 7am
Pendleside Events, 077 9626 6573

Top of Sorley Brow (A59)
GISBURN, CLITHEROE
Sundays (April-November)
077 1183 3543

Fleamarket
Station Rd
CLITHEROE
Fridays, 9am-4.30pm
01200 443012

Indoor Car Boot
Colne Leisure Centre, Albert Rd
COLNE
Sundays (October-May), 8.30am
Buyers from 9.30am-12.30pm
No new goods
01282 815756 / 077 1432 5614

Indoor Car Boot
Grimshaw St/Springvale Rd (Off A666)
DARWEN
Sundays (year-round), 8am, buyers from 9am
No number listed

Indoor Car Boot
Fleetwood YMCA Leisure Centre
The Esplanade
FLEETWOOD
Every other Sunday (September-Easter), 8am
Book in advance
079 8435 5264

Indoor and Outdoor Car Boot
Lancaster Auction Mart, Wyresdale Rd

LANCASTER
Sundays (year-round), 7am
DW Promotions, 079 4685 7010

Outdoor Fleamarket
Market Hall, Gas Street
LEIGH
Mondays-Wednesdays, 9am-4pm
01942 262018

Indoor and Outdoor Car Boot
Equestrian Centre, Ulnes Walton Lane
ECCLESTON, LEYLAND
Wednesdays (year-round), 7am
079 3158 4915

Outdoor Fleamarket
Rochdale
MIDDLETON
Tuesdays and some Saturdays
01706 864114

Hard-standing Car Boot
Vale of Lune Rugby Club, Torrisholme Rd
MORECAMBE
Sundays, 6.30am
01524 854742

Hard-standing Car Boot
Morecambe College, Morecambe Rd
MORECAMBE
Sundays (from April), 7am
Sports Coaching College, 077 5137 2929

Westgate Wanderers Football Club
Heysham Rd
MORECAMBE
Sundays (end-May-August), 8am
Wanderers Club, 077 5137 2929

Fleamarket
Tommyfield Market, Albion St
OLDHAM
Sundays, 6am-1pm
Wednesdays, 9am-3.30pm
0161 911 4515

Bric-a-brac Market
Clitheroe St
PADIHAM
Thursdays, 9am-4pm
01282 664651

Fairholme Car Boot
Fairholme Giant

Shard Lane
HAMBLETON, POULTON-LE-FYLDE
Saturdays and Sundays
(end-March-October), 7am
077 0299 8091

West Coast Indoor Car Boot
Wyrefield Rd, Off Bracewell Ave
POULTON-LE-FYLDE
Sundays (September-April), 6.30am
Buyers from 7.30am
Pre-booking available
DW Promotions, 079 4685 7010

Car Boot & Market
Victorian Open Market, Earl St
PRESTON
Tuesdays and Thursdays, 8am-3pm
Set up 6am
No food traders
Preston City Council, 01772 906048

Hard-standing Car Boot
Great Birchwood Country Park, Lytham Rd
(Off A584)
WARTON, PRESTON
Sundays, 8am
No number listed

Under-cover Dryden Car Boot
Manchester Rd
PRESTON
Sundays (year-round), 5am
Buyers from 5.30am
01772 225 0131 / 078 3421 1163

Car Boot
Railway St
RAMSBOTTOM
Sundays, 8am-3pm
Bury Markets, 0161 253 6520

Fleamarket
Railway St
RAMSBOTTOM
Wednesdays, Fridays and Saturdays, 8am-3pm
Bury Markets, 0161 253 6520

Indoor Car Boot
The Maze, Shakespeare St
SOUTHPORT
Every day except Bank Holidays (year-round)
10am
01704 884199

Mere Brow (Off A565)
Nr TARLTON
Sundays, 7am
079 3158 4915

Lambs Rd
THORNTON
Sundays (April-end of summer), 7am
DW Promotions, 079 4685 7010

Norcross Car Boot
Norcross Cleveleys, Norcross
Lane/Amounnderness Way
CLEVELEYS, THORNTON-CLEVELEYS
Saturdays (May-October), 7am
077 0299 8091

Birkenhead Market, Birkenhead Rd
MEOLS, WIRRAL
Wednesdays and Saturdays (year-round), 8am
Buyers from 9am
No number listed

LEICESTERSHIRE

Broomleys Farm, Broomleys Rd
COALVILLE
Sundays
01530 812992 / 079 7166 0772

Broughton Rd, B4114 Coventry Rd
CROFT
Sundays and Bank Holiday Mondays, 7am
01455 283420

Moira Car Boot
Moira Miners Sports Club (Off A44)
MOIRA, DONISTHORPE
Sundays, 9am
01283 548024

Bottesford, (Off A52)
Nr BOTTESFORD VILLAGE
Sundays, 9am
01283 548024 / 078 8008 1669

Croft Car Boot
Broughton Rd
STONEY STANTON, LEICESTER
Sundays and Bank Holiday Mondays (March-October), 6.30am, buyers from 7.30am
Occasional Saturdays, 11am
At the time of writing, Saturday car boots have been

postponed
01455 283420 / www.croftcarboot.com

Newbold Vernon Car Boot
Equestrian Centre, Barleston Rd
NEWBOLD VERNON, LEICESTER
Saturdays and Bank Holiday Mondays (end-May-October), 7am
077 9245 4563

Outdoor and Under-cover Car Boot
The Cattle Market, Scalford Rd
MELTON MOWBRAY
Sundays (year-round), 7.30am
Buyers from 8.30am-1pm
Tuesdays (antiques market), 7am-2pm
0115 921 3841 / 079 4734 8458

Quorn Car Boot
Granite Way
MOUNTSORREL
Sundays (March-October), 6.30am
Buyers from 7.30am
No number listed

Kibworth to Fleckney Rd, Kibworth Rd
SADDINGTON
Sundays and some Bank Holiday
Mondays, 7am
No food traders
Regency Fairs, 0116 240 2206 / 078 6620 8465 /
www.carbootinfo.com

Off A42 (signposts from Coalville)
MEASHAM, SWADLINCOTE
Sundays (year-round), 7.30am
Buyers from 8am-4pm
*Held in Swadlincote Market Hall during wet
weather and the winter months*
077 4705 2878

LINCOLNSHIRE

Next to Pennells Garden Centre
Humberston Rd
CLEETHORPES
Wednesdays and Saturdays (June-August)
079 4006 8539

Friends of Sidney Park Car Boot
Sidney Park, Brereton Ave
CLEETHORPES

Sundays (from mid-May for 14 weeks), 8.30am
01472 238322

Indoor and Outdoor Car Boot and Market
RAF Hemswell, Nr Caenby Corner
GAINSBOROUGH
Sundays and Bank Holiday Mondays (year-round), 6.30am-3pm
Close to the huge Hemswell Antiques Centre
01673 818240 / www.hemswellmarket.co.uk

Morrisons Car Boot
Field Next to Morrisons, Laceby Bypass
GRIMSBY
Sundays (April-September), 6am
No number listed

Scout Hut, Corner of Carr Lane-Cooper Rd
GRIMSBY
Saturdays (Feb-Nov)
Held inside in wet weather. Bring your own table or rent one for £1
01472 358911

Grange Farm, Brandon Rd
HOUGHAM
Saturdays and Good Friday, 8am
01400 250251 / 079 399 16968

Playing Field Assoc Car Boot
North Scarle, Swinderby Rd
NORTH SCARLE, LINCOLN
Every other Sunday (End-March-October), 7am
No number listed

Afternoon Car Boot
Little London Caravan Park (A156)
TORKSEY, LINCOLN
Saturdays and Wednesdays, 12pm
01427 718322

Grimoldby Cricket Club Car Boot
Tank Entrance of Manby Airfield, Manby
Middlegate
MANBY, LOUTH
One Sunday a month (April-September), 7am
Buyers from 9am
No set pattern of dates
07 327500

n, Main Rd
ET, LOUTH
ays (April-September), 7am
9am
f dates

078 3636 3723

Hard-standing Glanford Park Car Boot
Scunthorpe United Football Club
Doncaster Rd
SCUNTHORPE
Sundays (year-round), 6am, buyers from 7am
079 6782 1710

Normanby Raceway Car Boot
Normanby Rd
SCUNTHORPE
Saturdays (year-round), 7am
Buyers from 8am
075 0673 6410

Skegness Town Football Ground, Burgh Rd
SKEGNESS
Sundays (March-October), 7am
Buyers from 8am
Held on the football ground for 14 weeks, then moved to nearby St Clements sports field for another 14 weeks
077 9476 3791

Lay-by Car Boot
In the Field by Southview Leis, Burgh Rd
SKEGNESS
Saturdays (May-October), 6am
No number listed

Burgh Grand Car Boot
Burgh Le Marsh Sports Field
SKEGNESS
Thursdays and Bank Holidays, 7am
077 3256 9408

Pointon Car Boot
The Playing Field, Fen Rd
POINTON, SLEAFORD
Bank Holiday Mondays, 7am
Pointon Social Club, 078 0357 4063

Sleaford Town Football Club, Eslaforde Park,
Boston Rd
SLEAFORD
Some Sundays (May-August), 7am
No set pattern of dates
No number listed

Sleaford Sports Assoc, 01529 307197
Woodhall Spa Showfield, Jubilee Park
WOODHALL SPA
Sundays (June-November), 9am
No number listed

LONDON

Hard-standing Afternoon Car Boot
Battersea Technology College, Dagnall St
Entrance, Off Battersea Park Rd
BATTERSEA
Sundays (year-round), 12pm
Advance bookings only
079 4138 3588

Bounds Green Schools, Bounds Green Rd,
Opposite BG Tube Station
BOUNDS GREEN
Sundays and Bank Holiday Mondays, 12.30pm
Buyers from 1.30pm-5.30pm
Giant Car Boots, 020 8365 3000

Comber Grove Primary School, Comber Grove
CAMBERWELL
Saturdays (starts March), 8am
020 7703 4448

Sedgehill Field, Sedgehill Rd
CATFORD
Sundays, 10am, buyers from 11am
No number listed

Meridian Club, Charlton Park Lane
CHARLTON
Saturdays, 7am
No food traders
020 8856 1923

Chiswick Community School, Burlington Lane
CHISWICK
1st Sunday of the month, 6.30am-1pm
No new goods or market traders
No number listed

Afternoon Car Boot
Rosendale School, Rosendale Rd
DULWICH
Saturdays, 12pm (set up from 11am)
No number listed

Christchurch, New Broadway
EALING
Saturdays, 10am-2pm
020 8728 1346

Hard-standing Car Boot
Gas Board Sports Grounds, Corner of
Burgess Rd-Southend Rd
EAST HAM
Sundays (year-round), 8am

Bootilicious Car Boots, 077 5980 2675

Indoor Fleamarket
Sheen Lane Centre
EAST SHEEN
Fridays, 9am-1pm
Advance bookings only
020 8393 2042

Kingsmead School, Southbury Rd
ENFIELD
Saturdays (year-round), 7am, buyers from 8am
020 8351 5000

Radio Marathon Centre, Turkey St
ENFIELD
Saturdays (year round), 8am, buyers from 9am
Turkey St Market, 078 6404 5900

Opposite Odeon Cinema, Holloway Rd
Entrance behind McDonald's, Bowman's Place
FINSBURY
Saturdays, 8am
Sundays, 10.30am
01992 717198

Afternoon Car Boot
Christchurch School, Blackhall Lane
GREENWICH
Saturdays (irregular), 1pm (set up from 12pm)
020 8309 5696

Car Boot and Market
Holloway Rd, Grafton
HOLLOWAY
Saturdays, 8am-4pm (set up from 8am)
Sundays, 10am-2.30pm (set up from 10am)
01992 717198

Market Place, Marks Gate (A12)
ILFORD
Thursdays (March-September), 5am
Buyers from 7am
No number listed

Canonbury School, Canonbury Rd
ISLINGTON
Sundays (April-December), 7.30am
079 4024 1206

St Augustine's School, Broad Lane
KILBURN
Saturdays, 11am-3pm
No vans
020 8440 0170

University Hospital, High St
LEWISHAM
Saturdays, 7am
No number listed

Peckham Multi-storey Car Park
PECKHAM
Sundays, 6am
No number listed

Fisher Athletic Football Club, Off Salter Rd
ROTHERHITHE
Sundays, set up from 11am
020 8309 5696

Tottenham Community Sports Centre Car Parks
TOTTENHAM
Thursdays (year-round), 7am-2pm
Countryside Promotions, 01992 468619
www.countrysidepromotions.co.uk

New Covent Garden, Nine Elms
VAUXHALL
Sundays, 7am-2pm
No number listed

William Morris School, Folly Lane
Off Billet Rd (B179)
WALTHAMSTOW
Sundays (year-round), 8am-2pm
079 3291 9707

Hard-standing Car Boot
Winbledon Greyhound Stadium, Plough Lane
WIMBLEDON
Saturdays, Good Friday and Bank Holiday
Mondays (year-round), 7am
Wednesdays, 10.30am
Do not arrive before 7am for any of the days
01932 355538

Merton Abbey Primary School, High Path
SOUTH WIMBLEDON
Last Sunday of the month, 8am
No number listed

New River Sports Centre, White Hart Lane
WOOD GREEN
Fridays (year-round), 6am-2pm
Countryside Promotions, 01992 468619
www.countrysidepromotions.co.uk

Nightingale School, Bounds Green Rd
WOOD GREEN
Sundays (year-round), 6am

Buyers from 7am-1pm
Giant Car Boot Sales, 020 8365 3000

MERSEYSIDE

To be a regular seller at car boots in this county, you need to register with Trading Standards (see p113 for more details)

Stanley Rd
BOOTLE, LIVERPOOL
Sundays (year-round), 6am
0151 259 6873 / 079 3284 4130

Carnegie Rd, Off Green Lane
OLD SWAN, LIVERPOOL
Sundays (year-round), 6am
No food to be sold
0151 228 5626

Indoor and Outdoor Car Boot and Market
Tuebrook Market, West Derby Rd
Next to the Police Station
LIVERPOOL
Thursdays and Saturdays, 7.30am
0151 260 6352 / 078 6096 1660

Liverpool Cricket Club, Riversdale Rd
LIVERPOOL
Sundays (May-August), 9.30am
Buyers from 10.30am
0151 429 2930
www.liverpoolcricketclub.co.uk

Indoor and Outdoor Car Boot
Chalon Way Multi-storey Car Park
ST HELENS
Sundays (year-round), 6am
01744 677159

West Kirby Football Club, Greenbank Rd
WEST KIRBY, WIRRAL
Sundays (March-October), 7am
Buyers from 8am
No new goods, no food
079 3948 6441

MIDDLESEX

Hard-standing Under-cover Car Boot
Burnt Oak Station, Watling Ave
BURNT OAK, EDGWARE
Saturdays (year-round), 7.30am-4.30pm

Next to Burnt Oak Station
079 8398 7952 / www.watlingmarket.co.uk

Arches Field, Edgware Way, Spur Rd
Roundabout (A41)
EDGWARE
Sundays (Easter-September), 6am
Buyers from 7am
020 8578 5720 / 079 3253 2421

Hayes Football Club, Church Rd
HAYES
Wednesdays and Fridays, 8am-2pm
Advance bookings only
01494 520513 / 079 4758 0885

Hounslow Heath Garden Centre
HOUNSLOW
Saturdays and Sundays, 7am-1pm
Ring before travelling
020 8890 3485

Hounslow West Station Car Park
HOUNSLOW
Saturdays and Sundays, 7am-2pm
Bray Assoco, 01895 639912

Car Boot – Under-cover If Wet
Secondary School, Potter St
NORTHWOOD
Sundays, 8am
079 3153 9282

MIDLOTHIAN

To be a regular seller at car boots in this
county (and the whole of Scotland), you
need to register with Trading Standards
(see p113 for more details)

Woolworths Car Park, Milton Rd
EDINBURGH
Last Sunday of the month
(February-October), 7am
Rotary Club of Portobello, 077 8922 0583

Omni Car Boot
Greenside Place Multi-storey Car Park,
Greenside Place
EDINBURGH
Sundays (year-round), 8.30am
No number listed

MONTGOMERYSHIRE

See also Powys

Car Boot & Market
Harry Tuffins Supermarket
CHURCHSTOKE
Sundays, 7am
01588 620226

Abermule Community Centre (Off A483)
ABERMULE, MONTGOMERY
Some Saturdays (end-April-September), 7am
See website for dates
Abermule Community Centre, 01686 630240
www.abermule.cc

MORAYSHIRE

To be a regular seller at car boots in this
county (and the whole of Scotland), you
need to register with Trading Standards
(see p113 for more details)

Elgin Market, New Elgin Rd
ELGIN
Saturdays, 10am
01343 547047

Inchberry Car Boot
Mosstodloch to Rothes Rd
ORTON, FOCHABERS
Last Sunday of the month
(March-September), 7am
No number listed

NORFOLK

Late Morning Car Boot
Burgh Rd (A140)
AYLESHAM
Saturdays (Easter-October), 9am
Buyers from 11am
Strictly no buyers until 11am. No dogs on site
077 9696 4653

Banham Zoo, Kenninghall Rd
BANHAM
Sundays, 7am
No number listed

A149, nr Cromer
EAST RUNTON
Saturdays, 7am, buyers from 9am-2pm
Wednesdays, 3pm
077 9948 8292

Jules Car Boot
Market Rd, Burgh Castle
GREAT YARMOUTH
Sundays (March-September), 6am
01493 780015

Arminghall
LAKENHAM
Sundays, 1pm-4pm
Wednesdays, 9am-1pm
Chris Chambers, 01603 424899

Lingwood Sports Ground, Station Rd (Off A47)
LINGWOOD
Fridays (May-September), 6am
Buyers from 9am
Chris Chambers, 01603 424899

Longham Car Boot
Longham Village Hall, Chapel Rd
BRECKLAND, LONGHAM
Saturdays (June-October), 9.30am
01362 687015

Lukes Car Boot
Upper Flowerpot Lane, Stratton Rd
LONGSTRATTON
Saturdays (April-August), 7am
Buyers from 9am
077 7096 4307

Afternoon Car Boot
North Walsham Football Club, Green Rd
NORTH WALSHAM
Sundays and Thursdays (April-October), 11am
Buyers from 12pm
077 4820 9695

Arminghall Car Boot
Arminghall Site, Old Stoke Rd
ARMINGHALL, NORWICH
Sundays (March-November), 11.30am
Wednesdays (March-November), 7am
Buyers from 9am
Chris and Billy Chambers, 01603 424899

Costessey Park and Ride
NORWICH
Sundays (year-round apart from Christmas and
New Year), 6am
078 2433 2114

Hellesdon High School, Middletons Lane
HELLESDON, NORWICH
Saturdays (April-September), 7am
Buyers from 9am-1pm
No dogs
Chris Chambers, 01603 424899

Ali's Car Boot
Decoy Rd
ORMESBY ST MICHAEL
Every other Saturday (April-autumn), 8am
No number listed

Stalham Town Football Club, Rivers Park
Steppingstone Lane
STALHAM
Sundays, Fridays and Bank Holidays (spring-
November), 9am, buyers from 11am
077 9696 4653

NORTHAMPTONSHIRE

Holcot Showground, Poplar Farm, Poplar Lane
HOLCOT
Saturdays (starts April), 12pm
01604 781253 / www.holcot-showground.co.uk

Hard-standing Car Boot
Rushden & Diamonds Football Ground
Nene Park Stadium
IRTHINGBOROUGH
Sundays (year-round), 6am
Buyers from 7am-1pm
Rushden & Diamonds Football Club
01933 652000

Wicksteed Park, Barton Rd
KETTERING
Sundays (March-October), 7am
No food or drink
08700 621193 / www.wicksteedpark.co.uk

Duston Mill, Upton Way
NORTHAMPTON
Every 3rd Saturday of the month
(April-October), 8am
Buyers from 10am
No market traders
077 9061 8006 / www.dustonmill.co.uk

Flore Playing Field, Spring Lane
FLORE, NORTHAMPTON
Sundays (May-September), 6am
Buyers from 9am
No number listed

Little Billing Car Boot
Hub Farm, Green Land South
NORTHAMPTON
Sundays, 8am, buyers from 12pm
074 0367 9349

Hard-standing Car Boot
Northampton Town Football Club, Sixfields
Stadium, Upton Way
NORTHAMPTON
Last Sunday of the month, 9am
Buyers from 10am
No market traders
Northampton Town Supporters Trust
01604 499534 / www.ntfctrust.co.uk

Dale End Park, Croyland Rd
WELLINGBOROUGII
Every other Saturday, 7am
079 1081 1060

Mad Mile Car Boot
Park Farm Industrial Estate
WELLINGBOROUGH
Sundays and Bank Holiday Mondays
(April-October), 6am
Buyers from 7.30am
No number listed

Outdoor Fleamarket
Market Place
WELLINGBOROUGH
Tuesdays, 7am-3pm
Countrywide, 0800 358 3434

NORTHUMBERLAND

Scremeston Car Boot
The Marshall Outdoor Centre, Scremeston
BERWICK-UPON-TWEED
Sundays (year-round), 9am, buyers from 10am
Marshalls Outdoors, 01289 309090

Hexham Auction Mart, Tyne Green
HEXHAM
Sundays (February-November), 10.30am
Buyers from 12pm
No number listed

Afternoon Car Boot
Tranwell Airfield, Morpeth to Ponteland Rd
(B6524)
MORPETH
Sundays, 12pm, buyers from 1pm
Noble Promotions, 0191 586 8131
www.noble-promotions.homecall.co.uk

Wellfield, Earlsdon Rd
WEST MONKSEATON, WHITLEY BAY
Sundays, 7.30am, buyers from 8.30am
Noble Promotions, 0191 586 8131
www.noble-promotions.homecall.co.uk

The Fenton Centre, West Fenton
WOOLER
2nd Sunday of the month (May-September),
9.30am, buyers from 11am-3pm
*No food. Advanced booking recommended. Set in
parkland*
The Fenton Centre, 01668 216216

NOTTINGHAMSHIRE

Outdoor Fleamarket
Market Place
ARNOLD
Mondays, 8am
Wednesdays, 6pm
0115 920 1106

Shilo Way, Awsworth-Ilkeston Bypass
AWSWORTH
Sundays (May-November), 6.30am
Buyers from 8am
Blue Sky Promotions, 079 7348 1578
www.blueskycarboots.com

Outdoor Fleamarket
Market Place
BULWELL
Wednesdays
Firthdene, 0113 289 2894

Winbush Lane (A614)
CALVERTON
Sundays (year-round), 7am
Buyers from 10am-2pm
All-weather site
Jade Promotions, 078 0290 8183
www.calvertoncarboot.co.uk

Sherwood Forest Farm Park
EDWINSTOWE

Sundays, 7am-1pm
Treasure Trove, 01623 629219

Afternoon Car Boot
Leake Rd
GOTHAM
Sundays and Bank Holiday Mondays, 9am
Buyers from 1pm
SRB Promotions, 078 3354 3747

Hucknall Lane
HUCKNALL
Sundays and Holiday Mondays
No number listed

Outdoor Fleamarket
Market Place
LONG EATON
Tuesdays, 8am-4pm
Firthdene, 0113 289 2894

Indoor Car Boot
Botany Commercial Park
MANSFIELD
Sundays, 9.45am-12pm
Advance booking only
Treasure Trove, 01623 629219

Shirebrook Car Boot
Shirebrook Market Place, Station Rd
SHIREBROOK, MANSFIELD
Tuesdays, Wednesdays and Saturdays
(year-round), 7.30am
Bolsover District Council
01623 463073 / 079 7936 5685

Indoor Car Boot
The Market Pub, 43, High St
WARSOP, MANSFIELD
Sundays (November-March), 10am
Advance booking recommended
The Market, 01623 844673 / 842105

Outdoor Fleamarket
Market Place
NEWARK
Mondays and Thursdays, 8am-4pm
01636 655721

Indoor Car Boot
Clifton Leisure Centre, Southchurch Drive
NOTTINGHAM
Sundays (October-late-March), 7am
Buyers from 8.30am-12.30pm
Copperfield Fairs, 079 7191 4790

Indoor Car Boot
Greasley Sports Centre, Dovecote Rd
NEWTHROPE, NOTTINGHAM
2nd Sunday of the month (year-round), 7.30am
Buyers from 8.30am
01773 318136

Jaguar Car Boots
Hickings Lane
STAPLEFORD, NOTTINGHAM
Last Sunday of the month
(April-September), 9am
Buyers from 10.30am
079 2586 6451

Nottingham Racecourse
NOTTINGHAM
Sundays
0115 915 6970

Car Boot & Market
A634 Oldcotes to Blythe Rd (off A1)
OLDCOTES
Sundays and Bank Holiday Mondays
5am-3pm
01909 591008

Miners Welfare, Chesterfield Rd
PLEASLEY
Saturdays, 8am-1pm
Treasure Trove, 01623 629219

Nottingham to Mansfield Rd (A60)
RAVENSHEAD
Thursdays, 9.30am, buyers from 11am
No arrivals before 9.30am
Blue Sky Promotions, 079 7348 1578
www.blueskycarboots.com

Outdoor Fleamarket
Market Place
SUTTON IN ASHFIELD
Mondays, 8am-3pm
01623 551385

Cossall Rd (Off A609)
TROWELL
Sundays (June-October), 6.30am
Als Promotions, 077 3990 3580

Outdoor Fleamarket
Market Place
WORKSOP
Tuesdays, 8am-3pm
01623 551385

ORKNEY

To be a regular seller at car boots in this county (and the whole of Scotland), you need to register with Trading Standards (see p113 for more details)

Dounby Centre
DOUNBY
1st Sunday of the month, 1pm
01856 771280 / 721381

OXFORDSHIRE

Peachcroft Farm, Twelve Acre Drive
PEACHCROFT, ABINGDON
Sundays and Bank Holidays (April-November)
9am, buyers from 10am
Mega Boots, 01235 861049 / 079 2152 6769

Culham Site
ABINGDON
Saturdays, 9am, buyers from 10am
Mega Boots, 01235 861049 / 079 2152 6769

Bodicote Flyover Farm Shop, White Post Rd,
Nr Oxford Rd
BANBURY
Every other Sunday (April-October), 7am
01295 273608

Peter's Paddock, Bicester to Thame Rd (B4011)
BLACKTHORN, BICESTER
Sundays (starts April), 10.30am
Buyers from 1pm
077 8660 7097

Bicester Giant Car Boot
Stoke Lyn Rd
Nr CAVERSFIELD, BICESTER
Sundays and Bank Holiday Mondays
(Easter-November), 7am
Buyers from 8am
Mega Boots, 01235 861049 / 079 2152 6769

By Berinsfield Roundabout
Oxford to Henley Rd
BURCOT
Sundays and Bank Holiday Mondays
7am-2pm
Thames Valley Fairs, 01491 832196

Charlbury Cricket Club, Dyers Hill
Opposite the Station

CHARLBURY
1st Sunday of the month (May-September)
7am, buyers from 8.30am-12.30pm
Buyers are to park at the station, not in the club
The Committee, 079 0997 8863
www.charlburycricketclub.co.uk

Nr Abingdon
DRAYTON
Sundays and Bank Holiday Mondays, 7am
Buyers from 8am
Thames Valley Fairs, 01491 832196

Hard-standing Car Boot
Finmere Aerodrome (A421)
FINMERE
Saturdays, 8am-2pm
078 6064 3296

Oxsrad Sport and Leisure Centre
Court Place Farm, Marsh Lane
MARSTON
Last Sunday in the month, 9am
01865 741336

Car Free Indoor Car Boot
East Oxford Community Centre, 44b Princes St
Corner of Cowley Rd
OXFORD
Saturdays (from May), 9.30am
Buyers 10.30am-4.30pm
No number listed

Hard-standing Car Boot
Kassam Stadium, Grenoble Rd
GREATER LEYS, OXFORD
Sundays (year-round), 8am
Bray Assocs, 01895 639912

West Kidlington Primary School, Oxford Rd
KIDLINGTON, OXFORD
Sundays (March-summer), 7.30am
01865 460839

Off the A40
TETSWORTH
Every other Sunday (summer months), 7am
No number listed

Hard-standing Car Boot
Station Lane
WITNEY
Sundays (year-round), 7.30am
077 9135 9383

PERTHSHIRE

To be a regular seller at car boots in this county (and the whole of Scotland), you need to register with Trading Standards (see p113 for more details)

Errol Airfield
ERROL
Sundays, 8.30am-3pm
No food traders
01821 642940

St Johnston Football Club, McDiarmid Park, Crieff Rd
PERTH
Sundays, 9am
01738 459090

POWYS

See also Momtgomeryshire

Vulcan Arms (A470, nr Rhyader)
LLANWRTHWL
Saturdays, 9am
077 7230 6139

Cattle Market
RHYADER
Saturdays, 9am
01597 810340

SCOTTISH BORDERS

To be a regular seller at car boots in this county (and the whole of Scotland), you need to register with Trading Standards (see p113 for more details)

Car Boot & Market
The Racecourse
KELSO
Sundays (year-round), 8am, buyers from 9am
Spook Erections, 01386 765403
www.spookerection.com

Car Boot & Fleamarket
The Square
KELSO
First and last Wednesday of every month

(year-round), 9am
Buyers from 9.30am
No new items
Kelso Community Events, 01573 224687

SHROPSHIRE

Car Boot & Market
Whitburn St Car Park
BRIDGNORTH
Saturdays and Sundays, 7am
078 3150 6602

Car Boot & Market
Craven Arms, Newtown Rd (A489)
CHURCHSTOKE
Sundays, 10am-3pm
01588 620226

Table Top and Outdoor Car Boot
Church Aston Village Hall, Wallshead Way
CHURCH ASTON, NEWPORT
3rd Sunday of the month (year-round), 12pm
Buyers from 1pm
Bring your own table for the inside table top
Church Aston Village Hall, 01952 825258

SOMERSET

See also Bristol

Lansdown Hill, Next to the Racecourse
LANSDOWN, BATH
Sundays
No number listed

Plum Lane
BRIDGWATER
Sundays (April-September), 7am
079 7197 4616

Puriton Hill (Junction 23, M5)
PURITON, BRIDGEWATER
Saturdays (March-July), 7am
Buyers from 8am
14 weeks at Puriton Hill, then 14 weeks at Puriton Horse Rescue, Batch Rd
Puriton Horse Rescue, 077 3173 2907

Puriton Horse Rescue Centre, Batch Rd
PURITON, BRIDGEWATER
Saturdays (July-October), 7am

Buyers from 8am
Puriton Horse Rescue, 077 3173 2907

Afternoon Car Boot
BASC Sports Ground, Stoddens Rd
BURNHAM-ON-SEA
Saturdays (May-August), 12.30pm
Buyers from 2pm
No dogs
Paul's Promotions, 079 0062 1199

Oakmead Farm, Highridge Rd
EDITHMEAD, Nr BURNHAM-ON-SEA
Thursdays (May-October), 7am
No number listed

Winchester Farm, Wells Rd (A371)
CHEDDAR
Sundays (year-round), 6am
Buyers from 7.30am
01934 741378 / 078 31277 7327
www.cheddarcarboot.com

British Legion Car Boot
Opposite The Wood Pile (A38)
WEST HUNTSPILL, HIGHBRIDGE
Fridays (mid-April-late summer), 1pm
Buyers from 3pm
Pawlett Royal British Legion, 079 1944 1425

Midsomer Norton Rugby Club, Norton Down
Silver Street
MIDSOMER NORTON
Sundays (end-May-summer), 8am
Buyers from 9am
01761 472646

Ilchester Sports Field (Off the A37)
ILCHESTER
Sundays (April-October), 7am
Ilchester Sports Club, 079 6728 0754

Under-cover and Outdoor Car Boot
Standerwick Cattle Market, Between Bath and
Warminster (A36)
STANDERWICK
Sundays (year-round), 6.30am
Pied Piper Promotions, 01225 764890 / 079 5235
2931 / www.piedpiperpromotions.com

Bishop Fox's Community School, South Rd
TAUNTON
Sundays (January-March), 9am
Buyers from 10am

Paul's Promotions, 079 0062 1199

Evening Car Boot
St Augustines School, Lyngford Rd
PRIORSWOOD, TAUNTON
Fridays (May-September), 4.30pm
Buyers from 6pm
Paul's Promotions, 079 0062 1199

Prockters Farm, Blundell Lane
MONKTON HEATHFIELD, TAUNTON
Sundays and Bank Holiday Mondays (end-
March-November), 10am, buyers from 11am
Paul's Promotions, 079 0062 1199

Hard-standing Car Boot
Wellington Rugby Club, Corams Lane
ROCKWELL GREEN, WELLINGTON
Tuesdays (year-round), 8am, buyers from 9am
No number listed

Ancor Inn, Ancor Rd
WESTON-SUPER-MARE
Fridays and Saturdays (April-October), 7am
No number listed

Off Old A370
HEWISH, WESTON-SUPER-MARE
Sundays (June-September), 11am
Buyers from 12pm
078 1385 4541

Whitchurch Sports Centre, Heath Rd
WHITCHURCH
Saturdays (March-October), 12pm
01948 660660

Afternoon Car Boot
Yeovil Showground, Dorchester Rd (A37)
YEOVIL
Sundays, 11am, buyers from 1pm-4pm
079 7934 5914

STAFFORDSHIRE

Rugeley Rd
KINGS BROMLEY, BURTON-ON-TRENT
Saturdays (March-December), 7am
Buyers from 8am
Market traders can book pitches
Bromley Markets Ltd, 077 7909 1758

Brockton Car Boot
Off the A34

BROCKTON, CANNOCK
Sundays, 10am
077 9170 6175

Behind the Bowling Green Pub, Crossroads at
Leek Rd-Kingsley Rd (A520)
CELLARHEAD
Saturdays (year-round)
No number listed

Les Oakes' Car Boot
Oakamoor Rd
CHEADLE
2nd and last Sundays of the month (April-
November), 9am
*To book in advance, give your name and car
registration number*
Les Oakes & Sons, 01538 752126

Dark Lane
FEATHERSTONE
Sundays, 9am
01785 247695 / 078 3119 2116

Afternoon Car Boot
Collingwood Centre, Collingwood Drive
GREAT BARR
Saturdays and Sundays, 1.30pm
079 7497 0555

Creation Car Park, Etruria Rd
Next to Clough St Market
HANLEY
Sundays (year-round), 6am
Buyers from 7.30am
No number listed

Car Boot & Market
Cattle Market
LEEK
Sundays, 8.30am-1.30pm
079 6710 0297

Wood Farm, Wood End Lane
CURBOROUGH, LICHFIELD
Sundays (summer-autumn), 7am
Country Fairs, 01543 417878

Car Boot and Table Top
Audley & District Community Centre
Nantwich Rd
AUDLEY, NEWCASTLE-UNDER-LYME
1st Saturday of the month, 7.30am
Buyers from 9am
01782 723469
www.audleycommunitycentre.ik.com

The Stones, High St
NEWCASTLE-UNDER-LYME
Thursdays (year-round), 8am-3pm
Tuesdays (antiques & collectors market)
8am-3pm
Antique Forum, 01782 3936
www.antiqueforumgroup.com

Giant Car Boot & Market
Nr Tamworth
POLESWORTH
Bank Holiday Mondays, 9am-4pm
M & B 078 3188 4229

Stafford Common
STAFFORD
Sundays (March-December), 6am
Buyers from 7.30am
No number listed

Foxfield Steam Railway, Caverswall Rd Station
BLYTHE BRIDGE, STOKE-ON-TRENT
Tuesdays (year-round), 8am, buyers from 9am
077 4232 1924

Belfry-Fazeley Rd (A4091)
TAMWORTH
Sundays and Bank Holiday Mondays
(year-round), 7am
077 3656 0000 / 077 6730 6502
www.ebook.co.uk

Afternoon Car Boot
Car-Bar
KETTLEBROOK, TAMWORTH
Sundays, 4.15pm
No number listed

Kingsbury Rd (Junction 9, M42)
LEA MARSTON, TAMWORTH
Sundays and Bank Holiday Mondays
(year-round), 5.30am
No food traders, market traders to ring in advance
077 3656 0000 / 077 6730 6502
www.ebook.co.uk

Car Boot & Market
A4097, Junc 9 M42
LEA MARSTON
Sundays and Bank Holiday Mondays
7am-2pm
077 3656 0000 / 077 6730 6502
www.ebook.co.uk

Ashcroft Park, Stone Rd
BRAMSHALL, UTTOXETER

Sundays (May-September), 7am
01889 502508

Hill Farm, Bognop Rd
ESSINGTON, WOLVERHAMPTON
Sundays, 9am
077 9244 8370

Cannock Rd
SHARESHILL, WOLVERHAMPTON
Sundays, 1pm
077 9244 8370

STIRLINGSHIRE

To be a regular seller at car boots in this county (and the whole of Scotland), you need to register with Trading Standards (see p113 for more details)

Behind Rob Roy Visitor Centre
CALLANDER
Irregular Saturdays
No number listed

Kildean Market, Off Drip Rd (A84)
KILDEAN
Sundays, 9am
No number listed

SUFFOLK

Car Boot & Market
Banham Zoo, The Grove
BANHAM
Sundays, 7am
01953 715319

Barton Mills Village Hall, Mildenhall Rd
BARTON MILLS
Easter Bank Holiday Mondays, 7am
Barton Mills Village Hall
No number listed

Bartboots Car Boots
Opposite the old Sanfords Garden Centre
The Street
BARTON MILLS
Every other Sunday and Bank Holiday
Mondays (March-October), 8am-4pm
078 6071 6075 / www.bartboots.com

Harry's Farm, Next to Beck Row Golf Range
BECK ROW

Every other Saturday (May-November),
8am-4pm
078 6071 6075 / www.bartboots.com

Hard-standing Car Boot
Old Cavendish Site
FELIXSTOWE
Saturdays, 8am
Lions Club, 01294 286446

Royal British Legion, Mill Lane
FELIXSTOWE
Every other Saturday (late-July-November)
11am, buyers from 12pm
078 5659 0251

Grounds of the Taste of China Restaurant
Sturmer Rd (Off A1017)
NEW ENGLAND, HAVERHILL
Sundays (April-October), 8am
No market traders
078 7510 9448

Foxhall Stadium, Foxhall Rd
Sundays (March-June), 7am
IPSWICH
Shandale Ltd, 01473 403697

The Lions Club, Portman Rd Car Park
IPSWICH
Sundays (year-round), 6.30am-1pm
No market traders
The Lions Club, 078 6086 6587

Suffolk Showground, Felixstowe Rd (A1156)
IPSWICH
Sundays (July-September), 5.45am
Buyers from 6.15am
Shandale Ltd, 01473 403697

Kennett
KENNETT
Sundays (April-September), 7am
Buyers from 9am
No number listed

Car Boot & Market
Africa Alive Wildlife Park, Kessingland
LOWESTOFT
Sundays (February-October), 7.30am
Buyers from 8.30am
01953 715319

Melton Palying Field, Melton St
MELTON
1st Saturday of the month

(May-September), 7am
079 8561 8901

Indoor Fleamarket
Memorial Hall, High St
NEWMARKET
Tuesdays, 9.30am-4.30pm
01954 252329

Friday Street (A12)
BENHALL, SAXMUNDHAM
Every other Sunday (starts Easter), 6am
01394 410259

Stratford St Andrew Car Boot
The Riverside Centre
**STRATFORD ST ANDREW,
SAXMUNDHAM**
Every other Sunday (April-October), 7am
01728 602647

Indoor Car Boot
Stowupland Village Hall, Church Rd
STOWUPLAND
Some Sundays (January and March), 8.30am
Buyers from 9.30am
Advance booking necessary, not held all Sundays
Keith Moore, 01449 673499

Indoor and Outdoor Car Boot
Village Hall and Playing Field
A143 between Diss and Bury
WATTISFIELD
Some Sundays (May-August), 7am
Buyers from 8am
Only indoor pitches need to be booked in advance
Keith Moore, 01449 673499

Car Boot & Market
Bridge Farm
WOOLPIT
Sundays, 8am-2pm
01284 338 6228

SURREY

St Philomena's Catholic High School for Girls
Pound St
CARSHALTON
Last Sunday of the month
(March-October), 7am
020 8642 2025

Leg o'Mutton Playing Fields
Downside Bridge Rd

COBHAM
Some Sundays, all Bank Holiday Mondays
7.30am-4pm
Peter Marriott, 01372 724568

Cranleigh and District Lions Club, Cranleigh
Showground, Ewhurst Rd
CRANLEIGH
Some Sundays (May-August), 7.30am
Not every Sunday, see website for details
Cranleigh Lions 0845 833 2711
www.cranleighlions.org

Addington Park, Gravel Hill Rd
NR ADDINGTON VILLAGE, CROYDON
May Day Bank Holiday Monday, 7am
Buyers from 8am
Radio Mayday, 020 8689 9200

Royal Russell School, Coombe Lane
CROYDON
Every Mothering Sunday, 8am
Buyers from 9am
Royal Russell School Parents' Assoc
No number listed

Indoor Fleamarket
St Peters Hall, Ledbury Rd
CROYDON
Fridays, 7am-1pm
01883 622407

Mytchett Centre, Mytchett Rd (Off A321)
MYTCHETT, DEEPCUT
Thursdays and Saturdays (year-round), 8.30am
01252 657571

Hard-standing Car Boot
Station Car Park (A24)
DORKING
Sundays, 7am-1pm
Peter Marriott, 01372 724568

Imber Courts Sports Centre, Ember Lane
EAST MOLESEY
Some Sundays and Bank Holiday Mondays
(May-August), 8am
Peter Marriott, 01372 724568

Epsom General Hospital Staff Car Park
Dorking Rd
EPSOM
Some Sundays, 8am-12.30pm
No set pattern of dates
020 8337 8181

Hook Rd Arena, Chessington Rd, Hook Rd
EPSOM
Some Sundays, all Bank Holiday Mondays
(April-September), 7.30am-1pm
*No set pattern of dates. DVD and CD sales only by
prior arrangement with the organisers*
Peter Marriott, 01372 724568

Applegarth Farm
Grayshott to Borden Rd (B3002)
GRAYSHOTT
Saturdays, 11.30am, buyers from 12pm
01428 712777

Send Car Boot
Nuthill Fruit Farm, Portsmouth Rd (A3)
GUILDFORD
Sundays (April-September), 7.30am-1pm
01798 865703

Esher Rugby Club, Fieldcommon Farm, Waylan
Industrial Estate, Off Molesey Rd
HERSHAM VILLAGE
Sundays, 10am
020 8646 2814

Hard-standing Car Boot
Central Car Park, Consort Way East
Opposite Waitrose (Off A23)
HORLEY
Sundays, Good Friday and Bank Holiday
Mondays (March-December), 7am
Buyers from 8am
077 5405 4482

Tiffin School, Queen Elizabeth Rd
KINGSTON-UPON-THAMES
Some Sundays, 7.30am-1pm
No set pattern of dates
No number listed

Shooting Star Children's Hospice Grand Car Boot
Brenley Playing Fields, Tamworth Lane
MITCHAM
Every Other Sunday (July-October), 10.30am
020 8401 1071 / 078 1305 2539
www.shootingstar.org.uk

Nutberry Fruit Farm, Portsmouth Rd
RIPLEY
Sundays (April-September), 10am
079 7373 7806

Table Top Sale
Ripley Village Hall, Portsmouth Rd
RIPLEY

2nd Saturday of the month (year-round), 10am
No number listed

Field on New Rd, Opposite Queen Mary
Reservoir
SHEPPERTON
Saturdays (mid-May-September), 7.30am
Buyers from 8.30am
*No entry to selling area before 7.30am, no new
goods, no food*
Shepperton Car Boot, 078 0760 9283
www.sheppertoncarboot.co.uk

Shepperton Experience Car Boot
The Ranges, Chertsey Rd
SHEPPERTON
Sundays (May-August), 7am
*Tastings from local restaurants, entertainment and
arts and crafts, as well as car boot*
Ultimate Car Boots, 079 3923 6117

Hard-standing Car Boot
St Paul's Church, Thorpe Rd
EGHAM HYTHE, STAINES
1st Saturday of the month (February-October)
8am, buyers from 9am
No market traders
01784 452983

Table Top Sale
Thomas Wall Centre, Benhill Rd
SUTTON
Tuesdays (year-round), 6.30am-1pm
079 0414 2902

TS Puma Car Boot
Beddington Park, Church Rd
WALLINGTON
Some Sundays (May-September), 6.30am
Buyers from 7.30am
No set pattern of dates but one Sunday every month
Sutton Sea Cadets, 020 8669 8219

Hard-standing Car Boot
Hackbridge Primary School, Hackbridge Rd
WALLINGTON
Some Saturdays (April-October), 9.30am
No set pattern of dates. No food traders
020 8646 1948

Apps Court Farm, Hurst Rd
WALTON-ON-THAMES
Sundays (May-October), 7.30am
Apps Court Farm, 01932 244822
www.appscourtfarm.com

Warlingham Rugby Club, Limpsfield Rd
WARLINGHAM
Some Sundays and Bank Holidays Mondays
(May-August), 7am
No set pattern of dates
01883 622825

Bishop David Brown School, Albert Drive
WOKING
Last Saturday of the month (starts April), 10am
01932 349696

SUSSEX

Queensway
BOGNOR REGIS
Sundays, 8am-2pm
01243 827381

Brighton Racecourse
BRIGHTON
Some Sundays
No number listed

Hard-standing Car Boot
Brighton Railway Station
BRIGHTON
Sundays (year-round), 7am-2pm
Bray Assocs, 01895 639912

Afternoon Car Boot & Market
Cattle Market Site, Market Place
CHICHESTER
Sundays (year-round), 9.30am
Buyers from 12pm-4pm
Bray Assocs, 01895 639912

Treasure Island Table Top
British Car Auctions, Terminus Rd
CHICHESTER
Sundays (year-round), 9am-3pm
Tables provided, sale on 1st floor
No number listed

Fontwell Park Racecourse, Denmans Lane
FONTWELL
Sundays (year-round), 7am
01243 543335

Hard-standing Car Boot
Ford Airfield
FORD
Thursdays and Saturdays (year-round)

7.30am-2pm
No entry before 7.30am. No new goods, market traders or food sellers
078 5039 9781 / www.fordairfieldmarket.co.uk

Car Boot & Market
Market Place
HAILSHAM
Fridays, 5.30am
01323 844874

Hard-standing Car Boot
Ivyhouse Lane
HASTINGS
Sundays (year-round), 6.30am
No food or produce stalls
01424 812305 / 077 7551 8738

Carden School, Carden Hill
HOLLINGBURY
Sundays (April-September), 7am
078 8782 8031

Faygate (A264)
HORSHAM
Saturdays (starts May), 8am, buyers from 9am
020 8391 0638 / 078 1356 0204
www.horshamcarbootsale.co.uk

Badgers Farm, Selsey Rd
HUNSTON
Thursdays and Saturdays
(March-November), 7am
Buyers from 9am
01243 785001 / 078 5248 2011

Hard-standing Car Boot
Lancing Manor Leisure Centre, Manor Rd
LANCING
Saturdays (year-round), 7am-12pm
078 8934 2750

Hard-standing Car Boot
NCP Car Park, Lewes Precinct
Behind Waitrose
LEWES
Saturdays (year-round), 6am-2pm
No number listed

Indoor Table Top Sale
Grange Leisure Centre
MIDHURST
Saturdays, monthly 9.30am-12.30pm
01730 816841

The Dell (Off A259)
PEACEHAVEN
Every other Sunday, 7am
Different organisers fortnightly
No numbers listed

Hardriding Farm, Brighton Rd
Junction 11, M23
PEASE POTTAGE
Sundays (April-September), 7am-2pm
077 9913 5684
www.peasepottagecarbootsale.co.uk

Hard-standing Afternoon Car Boot
Plumpton Racecourse
PLUMPTON
Sundays (starts March), 12.30pm
01892 536575 / 077 9126 4655

Cophall Farm (A22)
POLEGATE
Sundays and Bank Holiday Mondays (April-October), 6am
Mammoth Boot Fairs, 01323 485676
www.mammothbootfairs.co.uk

Shaves Thatch/Poynings Car Boot
Opposite Ginger Fox, Henfield to
Brighton Rd (A281)
POYNINGS, HENFIELD
Some Sundays and some Bank Holiday
Mondays (March-September), 9.30am
Buyers from 10.30am
*Two Sundays on, two Sundays off – alternates with
Sayers Common car boot. Not in the village of
Poynings itself*
Mega Car Boot Sale, 01903 871221
www.megacarbootsale.co.uk

Toat Café, Slane St
PULBOROUGH
Sundays, 7am-12pm
01798 872911

Longhill School Car Park, Falmer Rd
ROTTINGDEAN
1st Saturday of the month, 9am-1pm
No dogs
PTFA, No number listed

Rottingdean Cricket Club
ROTTINGDEAN
Late spring and summer Bank Holiday
Mondays, 8am-4pm

Buyers from 9am-4pm
No number listed

*Hard-standing and Grass Afternoon Car Boot &
Market*
Newdigate Rd
RUSPER
Sundays (starts July), 1.30pm
Buyers from 2.30pm
01293 871002 / www.ruspercarbootsale.co.uk

Hickstead Car Boot
Opposite Hickstead Showground, Mill Lane
(B2118, off A23)
SAYERS COMMON
Some Sundays and some Bank Holiday
Mondays (March-September), 9.30am, buyers
from 10.30am
*Two Sundays on, two Sundays off – alternates with
Poynings car boot*
Mega Car Boot Sale, 01903 871221
www.megacarbootsale.co.uk

Shoreham Airport (A27)
SHOREHAM
Sundays (April-October), 6am
Buyers from 7.30am
No dogs
Shoreham Airport, 077 6774 6471

Shoreham Flyover, Steyning Rd
Junction of A238/A27
SHOREHAM
Sundays (spring-autumn), 7.30am
079 7025 7944

Hard-standing Car Boot
Co-op, Newlands Rd
WORTHING
Sundays (year-round), 7am
078 9908 2149

TYNE AND WEAR

*To be a regular seller at car boots in
Newcastle, you need to register with
Trading Standards (see p113 for more
details)*

St Oswald's Hospice, Regent Ave
GOSFORTH, NEWCASTLE-UPON-TYNE
Last Saturday of the month

(March-October), 7am
Buyers from 9am
St Oswald's Hospice, 0191 246 8123

Afternoon Car Boot
Linskill Community Centre, Linskill Terrace
NORTH SHIELDS
Saturdays (year-round), 12.30pm
Buyers from 1.30pm
0191 270 8298

Fleamarket
Metro Station
TYNEMOUTH
Sundays, 9am-4pm
0191 281 3803

Table Top Boot Sale
Burnside Community College, Junction of High
St and St Peter's Rd
WALLSEND
Sundays, 12.45pm, buyers from 1.30pm
Must be booked in advance. Tables provided
No number listed

Wellfield Car Boot
Earsdon Rd
WEST MONKSEATON, WHITLEY BAY
Sundays, 7am, buyers from 8am
Noble Promotions, 0191 586 8131
www.noble-promotions.homecall.co.uk

WARWICKSHIRE

Balsall Common Rugby Club
Kenilworth Rd (A4177)
BALSALL COMMON, BALSALL
Sundays, 8am
077 9692 8853

Nicholas Chamberlain School, Bulkington Rd
BEDWORTH
Some Sundays, 7am-1pm
One Sunday a month, no set pattern of dates
077 5995 5366

Smith's Field, Off Rugby Rd
BINLEY WOODS, BRANDON
Every other Sunday, Bank Holiday Mondays
8.30am-1pm
02476 543471

Furnace End Car Boot & Market
Coleshill / Nuneaton Rd (B4114)
FURNACE END, COLESHILL
Sundays, 8am-2pm
M & B Promotions
01827 897325 / 077 7581 3295

Indoor Car Boot
Howitzers Club, Albert St
COVENTRY
Saturdays (year-round), 10am
Buyers from 11am
Howitzers Club, 02476 222418

Mercia Hard-standing Car Boot
Mercia Leisure Park, Lockhurst Lane (B4118)
COVENTRY
Sundays, 8am
02476 456503

Old Coventrians Rugby Club, Tile Hill Lane
COVENTRY
Sundays (starts May), 7am-1pm
*Advance booking recommended on the Saturday at
the clubhouse*
No number listed

Warwick Rd (A4189)
HENLEY-IN-ARDEN
Wednesdays, Saturdays and Sundays
(year-round), 6am
Buyers from 7.30am
Advance booking recommended
077 1112 1211

CJ's Car Boot
Leamington Rugby Club, Moorefields
Kenilworth Rd
LEAMINGTON SPA
Sundays (May-August), 6am
Carol & John, 077 9527 8338
www.cjscarboot.co.uk

Long Itchington Car Boot
Marton Rd Farm, Marton Rd
LONG ITCHINGTON
Wednesdays (May-September), 10.30am
079 8931 3985
www.martonroadfarm.co.uk

Hard-standing Car Boot
Airfield, nr Stratford (off A4632)
LONG MARSDEN

Sundays, 6am, buyers from 7am
01827 892756

Coppice Lane
MIDDLETON, SUTTON COLDFIELD
Saturdays (year-round), 7am-3pm
077 3656 0000 / 077 6730 6502
www.ebook.co.uk

Hard-standing Car Boot
St Paul's Church of England Primary School
Wiclif Way
STOCKINGFORD, NUNEATON
Some Sundays (May-July), 7.30am
One Sunday a month, no set pattern of dates
No number listed

Indoor Fleamarket
United Reform Church, Chapel St
NUNEATON
Tuesdays and Fridays, 8.30am-3pm
01827 895899

Hard-standing Car Boot
North Warwickshire Sports Ground
Tamworth Rd
POLESWORTH
Sundays, 8am
No number listed

Alwyn Rd
DUNCHURCH, RUGBY
Saturdays (April-October)
No number listed

Hard-standing Car Boot
Rugby Town Football Club, Butlin Rd
Off Clifton Rd
RUGBY
Sundays, 7am, buyers from 8am
078 6509 4814

Stoneleigh Park (B4113)
STONELEIGH PARK
Sundays (September-April), 6am
Carol & John, 077 9527 8338
www.cjscarboot.co.uk

The Slough (A448)
STUDLEY
Sundays (April-October), 6am
No food
01527 892670

Hard-standing Car Boot
Warwick Corp of Drums Car Park
Hampton Rd
WARWICK
Sundays (April-October), 8am
No number listed

WEST LOTHIAN

To be a regular seller at car boots in this county (and the whole of Scotland), you need to register with Trading Standards (see p113 for more details)

Greyhound Track, Armadale Stadium
Bathgate Rd
ARMADALE
Sundays (year-round), 9am-1pm
079 0188 4184

Bathgate Open Air Market, Whitburn Rd
BATHGATE
Wednesdays, Fridays and Saturdays
(year-round), 10am-4pm
No number listed

WEST MIDLANDS

See Staffordshire, Warwickshire and Worcestershire

WILTSHIRE

Castle Combe Racing Circuit
CHIPPENHAM
Sundays, 9am-2pm
01249 782417

Old Dairy Farm, Main Rd
DAUNTSEY, CHIPPENHAM
Sundays (April-October), 7am
Buyers from 8am
01249 890291 / 079 7422 7340

Bric-a-brac Market
Market Place
CHIPPENHAM
Fridays and Saturdays
Hughmark, 0118 945 1799

Salisbury Fire Station, Ashley Rd
SALISBURY
1st Sunday of the month
(February-December), 7.30am
Buyers from 8.30am
01722 332211 / www.salisburyfirestation.info

Salisbury Racecourse, Drove Lane
SALISBURY
August Bank Holiday Monday, 6.30am
Buyers from 10am
Rotary Club of Wilton Charities, 01722 324681

Allweather Car Boot
Southern Counties Auctioneers, Livestock
Market, Salisbury Rd
NETHERHAMPTON, SALISBURY
Sundays (year-round), 6.30am
Buyers from 7.30am
078 9984 4929

Indoor Fleamarket
United Reform Church, Fisherton St
SALISBURY
Tuesdays, 8.30am-3pm
01202 669061

Blunsdon Stadium (Off A419)
BLUNSDON ST ANDREW, SWINDON
Saturdays, Sundays and Wednesdays, 7am
No number listed

Afternoon Car Boot
Chapel Farm, Bottom of Blunden Hill
BLUNSDON, SWINDON
Sundays, 12pm, buyers from 1pm
No number listed

Afternoon Hard-standing Car Boot
Link Leisure Centre, next to ASDA
SWINDON
Sundays and Good Friday, 1pm-4pm
ML Promotions, 078 6055 0380
www.mlpromotions.co.uk
swindonafternoon.htm

WIGTOWNSHIRE

To be a regular seller at car boots in this
county (and the whole of Scotland), you
need to register with Trading Standards
(see p113 for more details)

Indoor Car Boot/Table Top
The Millennium Centre, George St
STRANRAER
Last Sunday of the Month
(July-December), 9.30am-1.30pm
Check the website for other dates. Table provided
Wendy Jesson, 01776 706279
www.south-west-events.co.uk

WORCESTERSHIRE

See also Herefordshire

To be a regular seller at car boots in the
city of Worcester, you need to register
with Trading Standards (see p113 for
more details)

Wholesale Market, Pershore Rd
BIRMINGHAM
Sundays, 7am-2pm
0121 303 0250

Dared (A435)
BRANSONS CROSS
Saturdays (May-September), 6am
078 8507 7221 / www.daredcarboot.co.uk

Opposite the Queen's Head Pub, Sugarbrook
Lane (Off A38)
BROMSGROVE
Sundays, 7am, buyers from 10am
078 8507 7221 / www.daredcarboot.co.uk

Afternoon Car Boot
Behind the Country Girl Pub, Hanbury Rd
HANBURY, BROMSGROVE
Fridays, 3pm, buyers from 4pm
078 8507 7221 / www.arrowcarboot.co.uk

Afternoon Car Boot
By the Folly Pub, Rabbit Run, Between Dudley
and Telford (B4176)
DUDLEY
Saturdays, 12pm
078 9026 7041

Malvern Rugby Club, Spring Lane
MALVERN
Sundays, 1pm
Steve and Tracey, 077 9211 1947

Indoor and Outdoor Giant Fleamarket
3 Counties Showground
MALVERN
Irregular Sundays, Thursdays and Bank
Holiday Mondays, 7.30am-4pm
B & B, 077 7414 7197

Hoggs Lane
NORTHFIELD
Saturdays
079 3299 7713

Indoor and Outdoor Car Boot
Arrow Auctions, Bartleet Rd
WASHFORD, REDDITCH
Sundays (year-round), 7am, buyers from 9am
078 8507 7221 / www.arrowcarboot.co.uk

Afternoon Car Boot
Dripshill Farm, Guarlford Rd, Nr Malvern
RYDD
Sundays (March-September), 1pm
078 0063 9139

Highgate United Football Club
Tythe Barn Lane
SHIRLEY, SOLIHULL
Sundays and Bank Holiday Mondays
(May-August), 5.30am
Buyers from 8am
079 7371 8087

The Burgage, Off Teme St
TENBURY WELLS
Bank Holiday Mondays, 7am
078 8910 8206

Hard-standing Indoor and Outdoor Car Boot
Christopher Whitehead School, Malvern Rd
ST JOHNS, WORCESTER
Some Sundays (February-December), 12.45pm
Buyers from 1.15pm
No set pattern to dates
Steve and Tracey, 077 9211 1947

WREXHAM

Boot Sale & Market
Chirk Airfield, Junction A5 and A483, By the
McDonald's Roundabout

CHIRK
Sundays and Bank Holiday Mondays
(January-October), 5am-2pm
Chirk Airfield, 01691 773047
www.chirkairfield.co.uk

Bryn-Y-Grog, nr Wrexham
MARCHWIEL
Sundays, 7am
01978 266913

Greenhill
SOUTHWICK, TROWBRIDGE
Saturdays and Sundays (Easter-October), 7am
078 1042 8106

YORKSHIRE

*To be a regular seller at car boots in
Humberside, North Yorkshire and South
Yorkshire you need to register with
Trading Standards in all three areas (see
p113 for more details)*

Market Site
BARNSLEY
Sundays (year-round), 6am
Barnsley Council, 01226 772239

Bedale Park, Leyburn Rd
BEDALE
Saturdays (April-October), 6.30am
Bedale Town Council, 01677 427949

Hard-standing Indoor and Outdoor Car Boot
Bingley Auction Mart, Town Centre
BINGLEY
Sundays (year-round), 7.30am
01274 883137

Danes Wood Farm, Opposite Lynks
Golf Course
BRIDLINGTON
Sundays and Bank Holiday Mondays
(June-winter), 7am
BP Markets, 079 1394 5261

Daisy St Car Park
BRIGHOUSE
Sundays and Bank Holiday Mondays

(year-round), 6am, buyers from 7am
No new goods
01422 359034
www.calderdale.gov.uk/business/markets/car
-boot-sales.html

Market Place, Church Rd
DENABY
Sundays and Wednesdays (year-round), 4am
Buyers from 6am-1pm
Street Market Specialist, 0800 358 3434

Under-cover, Hard-standing Car Boot
Market Place
DEWSBURY
Sundays (year-round), 7am
01484 223730

Bric-a-brac Market
Market Place
DINNINGTON
Saturdays, 8am-3pm
01709 700 0072

Car Boot & Market
Keepmoat Stadium, Stadium Way
DONCASTER
Sundays, 6.30am
Keepmoat Stadium and Doncaster Council
01302 862480

The Bull Inn, Main St
GRISTHORPE, FILEY
Saturdays and Sundays
(Easter-end-October), 7.30am
077 4774 7718

Rising Sun Farm, Filey Rd
GRISTHORPE, FILEY
Tuesdays and Thursdays
(June-September), 7am
Countryside Markets Ltd, 01964 529239

Broad St Car Park
HALIFAX
Sundays and Bank Holiday Mondays
(year-round), 6am-1pm
01422 359034
www.calderdale.gov.uk/business/markets/car
-boot-sales.html

Outdoor Fleamarket
Piece Hall

HALIFAX
Thursdays, 9am-4pm
01422 321002

Ripley Cricket Club, Ripon Rd (A61)
RIPLEY, HARROGATE
Sundays, 7.30am, buyers from 8.30am-1pm
Ripley Cricket Club, 01483 223964

Pannal Junction, Junction of A61 and A658
PANNAL, HARROGATE
Sundays (March-October), 7am
079 4426 5562

Indoor Fleamarket
Holme Centre, Holme St
HEBDEN BRIDGE
Sundays, 9am-4.30pm
01422 823589

Second-hand Market
Valley Road, Town Centre
HEBDEN BRIDGE
Wednesdays, 9am-4pm
01422 359034

Brook St, Market Hall
HUDDERSFIELD
Tuesday, 9am-4pm
01484 223196

Car Boot & Market
Craven Park
MARFLEET, HULL
Saturdays (year-round), 6am, buyers from 7am
No number listed

Walton St
HULL
Sundays and Wednesdays (year-round), 6am
No number listed

Grange Moor, Nr Coal Museum
KIRKLEES
Sundays (July-August), 7am
No number listed

Pontefract Lane
LEEDS
Sundays (year-round), 6am
No number listed

Second-hand Market
Market Halls

MEXBOROUGH
Thursdays, 9am-4pm
01709 582036

Morley Rugby Football Club, Scatcherd Lane
MORLEY
1st Sunday of the month (May-September)
7.30am
Check website as it's not always the 1st Sunday
0113 253 3487
www.morleyrfc.co.uk/events_list.htm

Car Boot & Market
Wharfedale Farmers Auction Mart, Leeds Rd
OTLEY
Sundays (February-November), 10.30am
Buyers from 12pm
079 4426 5562

Pickering Showground (A169)
PICKERING
Most Sundays, 7am
*Note, as it's sometimes cancelled for other events,
the car boot is not every Sunday*
01751 473780

Fleamarket
Market Place
PICKERING
Saturdays and Sundays, 9am
01751 473780

Afternoon Car Boot
Ripon Racecourse, Boroughbridge Rd
RIPON
Sundays, 12pm, buyers from 1pm
Noble Promotions, 0191 586 8131
www.noble-promotions.homecall.co.uk

The Recreation Ground
NORTH STAINLEY, RIPON
Bank Holiday Mondays, 7am
Buyers from 8am
No number listed

Lebberston Car Boot
Opposite Esso Garage, Filey to Scarborough Rd
(A165)
LEBBERSTON, SCARBOROUGH
Sundays and Bank Holiday Mondays (Easter
September), 6.30am, buyers from 7.30am

Countryside Markets Ltd, 01964 529239

Indoor and Outdoor Car Boot
North Yorkshire Event Centre, Atley Hill Rd
SCORTON
Sundays (year-round), 7am, buyers from 8am
Wednesdays (year-round), 4pm
Buyers from 4.30pm
Under-cover during the winter
079 0990 4705

Smithfield Car Park, Nr Victoria Quays
SMITHFIELD, SHEFFIELD
Sundays, 7am
No vans
0114 273 5281
www.sheffieldmarkets.co.uk/markets.php

Riverside Field, Keighley Rd
SILSDEN
Some Sundays (April-July), 7am-1pm
No set pattern of dates
01535 654747

Next to Railway Station, High St
SOUTH ELMSALL
Thursdays (April-December), 7am
Wakefield Metropolitian District Council
01924 306090

Fleamarket
Sowerby Bridge
SOWERBY BRIDGE
Saturdays, 8am-3pm
01422 359034

Stokesley Showground
STOKESLEY
Bank Holiday Mondays (March-August), 7am
Buyers from 8am
No number listed

Indoor & Outdoor Car Boot
Thirsk Auction Mart, York Rd
(Junction A19/A168)
THIRSK
Sundays (year-round), 10am, buyers from 11am
DDF Fairs Ltd, 079 8658 3232

Car Boot & Market
Thirsk Racecourse, Ripon Rd
THIRSK

Sundays, 8.30am
Noble Promotions, 0191 586 8131
www.noble-promotions.homecall.co.uk

Outdoor Fleamarket
Town Centre
TODMORDEN
Thursdays, 9am-4pm
01706 819731

Market Site, Teall St
WAKEFIELD
Sundays, 5am-1pm
No market traders, no new goods
Wakefield Council, 01924 305907

Rufforth Park
WETHERBY
Sundays (year-round), 9am
Buyers from 10am-1pm
No number listed

Car Boot & Market
Wetherby Racecourse, York Rd
WETHERBY

Sundays, 7am, buyers from 8am
Northern Promotions, 0844 800 3394
wwwnorthernpromotions-fairs.co.uk

Wigginton Car Boot
Home Farm, Corban Lane
WIGGINTON, YORK
Sundays (April-October), 7am
01904 768463

Indoor & Outdoor Car Boot
York Auction Centre
MURTON, YORK
Sundays, 7am
01904 486713

York Racecourse
YORK
Saturdays, 7.30am
No new goods, no car boots when racing on
01429 881917

Publications and Websites

The Car Boot and Fairs Calendar contains a daily diary of car boot sales and appears bi-monthly, apart from the extra-sized winter issue (five issues a year). It's available from most large boot sales and antiques fairs or you can subscribe. Call 01981 251633, write to *The Car Boot and Fairs Calendar*, PO Box 277, Hereford, HR2 9AY or e-mail detailscarboot@aol.com for more information. You could alternatively subscribe to the website www.carbootcalendar.com for full listings.

Internet car boot sites

www.carbootjunction.co.uk – Useful website but not always up to date, with some listings for one-off events over a year old. But handy for regular car boots.

www.boot-fairs.co.uk – Very similar to Car Boot Junction. Tends to have more contact numbers but less car boots.

www.carbootsrus.com – Decent directory but I find it hard to read. A redesign would be a huge benefit as it has car boots not listed on other sites.

www.bootsaleforum.co.uk – Sponsored by iBootSale, it's not the most active site but worth keeping an eye on to see what boot sales are recommended, or otherwise.

Other ideas

Local press – see what's happening near you in your local paper or the free ads.

The *Friday Ads* is useful – find it free in shops, newsagents, libraries etc – or see www.friday-ad.co.uk.

Word of mouth – with thanks to all the booters who told me about all the car boots which are normally only listed in the local press (if even there).

Signposts – most car boots are signposted a day or two in advance close to the actual event, depending on the local council.

Car boots themselves – it can be that simple. I've discovered car boots with no advertising simply by being on the right road at the right time.

Is your car boot or favourite car boot not listed? Write to Fiona Shoop (CBS), Remember When, Pen & Sword Books Ltd, 47, Church St, Barnsley, S. Yorks, S70 2AS.

These listings are free, no organiser was charged any fee for entry in this book.

INDEX

Individual boot sales are noted in the directory by their county, not the index.